Black Heroes

Inspiring Stories of Resilience, Courage, and Triumph Against Adversity

Welcome Aboard, Check Out This Limited-Time Free Bonus!

Ahoy, reader! Welcome to the Ahoy Publications family, and thanks for snagging a copy of this book! Since you've chosen to join us on this journey, we'd like to offer you something special.

Check out the link below for a FREE e-book filled with delightful facts about American History.

But that's not all - you'll also have access to our exclusive email list with even more free e-books and insider knowledge. Well, what are ye waiting for? Click the link below to join and set sail toward exciting adventures in American History.

Access your bonus here
https://ahoypublications.com/
Or, Scan the QR code!

Table of Contents

Introduction

The media has given Black identity the ugly face paint of a criminal, thug, and clown. This dangerous misconception has put limitations on Black people across continents for many generations. When you wash off the paint and see the real faces of Black heroes worldwide, no distorted image can mislead you. Culture is created through traditions, shared identity, and stories. Passing on the narratives of the revolutionary lives of these Black heroes sown the seeds of empowerment. By keeping their memory alive, the deceptive fog of inaccurate depictions of global Africans is removed.

The history of Black people and the valiant bravery they have exhibited in the face of adversity is unparalleled. These cultural icons build the Colosseum of the Black experience, mastery, rebellion, and enrichment. Examining these historical giants can help humanity mirror the positive traits of their noteworthy lives. Their inspiring stories move even the hardest of hearts. Through their unbreakable courage and determination, they rise to stamp their names in the unbroken chain of the human story.

Telling the Black story reveals the greatness of African people in the diaspora and on the continent. The struggle of these heroes against their limitations and societal discrimination captures the essence of the unwavering human spirit. This beginner-friendly text comprehensively overviews legendary heroes like Maya Angelou, Dr. Martin Luther King Jr, and Harriet Tubman. By their actions, you can be inspired to keep the flames of progress burning and elevate it to an inferno.

This in-depth dive into their lives, struggles, and achievements acts as a beacon for their brilliance. Their contributions shifted the world and left a legacy that will stand tall through the ages. History awakens the teachings of the ancestors. Studying the lives of these great individuals sets a bar to aim for, as well as a milestone to surpass. The beauty of studying historical records is that humanity can collectively build on the wisdom of people who came before. The endless lessons in the inspirational lives of these Black heroes carve in stone the African contribution to shaping the modern world. The doors they have opened have improved society for many today, but through their tales, the baton is passed to the next generation.

Dive into the tumultuous journeys that shaped the legends of these unforgettable heroes. See yourself in their bravery, justice, determination, and intelligence. Exploring these stories unveils an emotional ride of triumphs and tribulations that formed some of the greatest historical narratives to ever move the needle of the globe. Through these stories, the global Africans' contributions to the world are set on a hill instead of being hidden in the darkness of miseducation.

Chapter 1: Defiant Voyager: The Harriet Tubman Odyssey

"I started with this idea in my head; There's two things I've got a right to, death or liberty."

- Harriet Tubman

The early 19th century was a time when dark clouds loomed over the United States... a nation, young and vibrant, which was tragically divided. During this time, millions of people were held captive in the monstrous institution of slavery by the Southern states, with no hope of freedom. This slavery business was like an incurable disease slowly killing the body of the nation; and a parasite on its soul, sucking its Black-life energy with reckless abandonment. It denied basic human rights to countless African Americans. Many of them were born into the slavery system, and families were separated, never to be united again during this time.

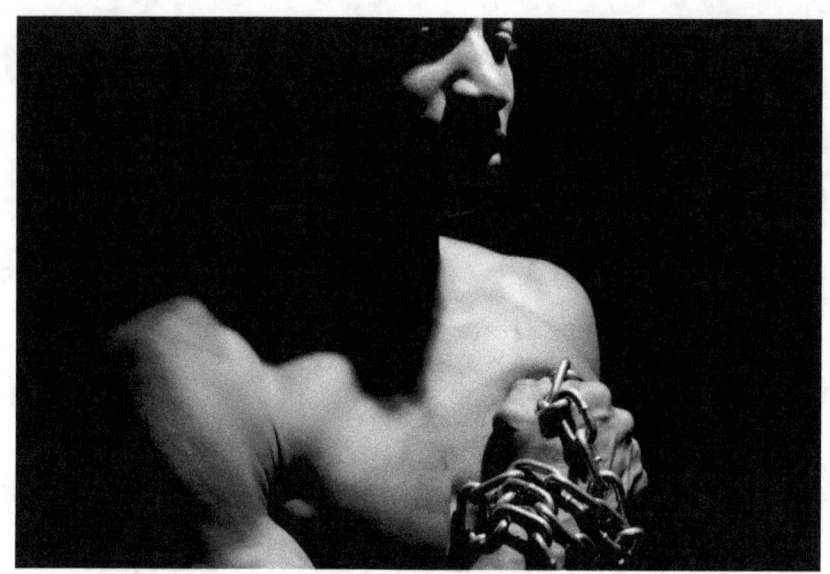

Slavery denied basic human rights to countless African Americans.
https://pixabay.com/photos/power-freedom-male-slavery-strong-5508643/

This was an era when people weren't seen as people at all. Men, women, and children were treated like objects, hauled around, and sold like meat and vegetables at the market. Their days weren't their own. They had no life except for what was asked of them. They had no choice but to do the backbreaking labor demanded by their owners. Fear hung heavily in the air as different generations of slaves moved about with hushed steps and bowed heads. At the sound of the whip, everyone was constantly reminded of the punishment that awaited any form of disobedience. This wasn't some far-off nightmare that they woke up from if they pinched themselves long enough. Not even gallons of teeth-clattering cold water wasn't about to wake them up to a warm smile or a peaceful room. This was the people's reality, the brutal reality of slavery.

But, while this darkness had a chokehold on the people, a flicker of hope was ignited, a flame that would later become a wildfire. Born into this harsh reality, around 1820 on the Eastern Shore of Maryland, Dorchester County, was a girl child who, as we later found out, was no doubt destined for greatness. The baby was named Araminta Ross. She was born into an enslaved family, with her parents being Ben and Rit Ross, both of which were owned by Anthony Thompson and Mary Pattison Brodess, respectively. The union of their owners brought the enslaved family together for as long as they could manage, with Harriet as the middle child of nine enslaved siblings.

A Child of Slavery

Right from an early age, Harriet was well acquainted with the definition of hardship. She was torn from her mother, who was assigned to serve in the dreaded "big house." Now left with no maternal care, Harriet became a mother to her siblings, even though she was barely a child. Most of her siblings were later sold off to different parts of the world by the Brodess family, who owned her and her family. Mary Brodess's son, Edward, sold three of Harriet's sisters far away, shattering their family bond. This wasn't the only time they tried to break them apart. A trader from Georgia even came looking to buy Harriet's little brother, Moses. But her mother, Rit, stood her ground. She wouldn't let them take another piece of her family. This brave act of defiance left a lasting impression on the young Harriet, showing her the power of fighting back.

At the tender age of five or six, she was ripped away again, forced to be a nursemaid for a cruel woman named "Miss Susan." Her nights at Miss Susan's home were filled with the constant threat of the whip's sting. She was usually assigned the task of rocking the baby of the house to sleep, and if at any point the baby wailed out like babies usually do, Harriet would squeeze her eyes shut at the thought of the punishment she was bound to receive for the unforgivable crime of a restless baby. Physical violence was as normal as people brushing their teeth daily for Harriet and her family. The whippings she usually got were brutal, leaving scars etched not just on her skin but on her soul. On a particular day, she was whipped five lashes, and these became tattooed on her skin for the rest of her life.

With her clever and defiant mind, Little Harriet soon found ways to resist her oppressors. She would disappear for days, sometimes just to get a fleeting taste of freedom. She would use several layers of clothing as a makeshift shield, a desperate attempt to ward off the coming blows and whips. Whenever she was pushed to the edge, she would fight back, roaring like a primal tiger, ready to devour someone down to the bone.

Harriet Tubman.

As Harriet got older, life didn't become any easier. She was again sent to work for another master. This time, it was a planter named James Cook. While working for Cook, the young girl barely got any break. It wasn't long before she was caught in the net of different illnesses due to her exposure to harsh weather conditions. Even when struck down by measles, she was forced to trudge through the marshes, checking traps. The illness affected her so much that it had to take her mother stepping in to nurse her young body to health. The reunion was a breath of fresh air for the child, but unfortunately, it didn't last. Soon after she recovered, she had to return to the brutal cycle of being hired out to different masters.

A Broken Skull with a Defiant Soul

Years passed by and Harriet grew stronger while her work grew even harsher. She spent most of her time in fields and out in the thickest forests, taming oxen, wrestling plows, and hauling logs that were as heavy as the burden of slavery on her shoulders. She executed her work with all the strength and diligence she could muster. She favored physical plantation work over the usual indoor domestic chores that were reserved for enslaved women at the time.

In 1835, a defining moment struck in Harriet's life. She had just turned thirteen years old. The little girl was sent to a dry goods store for supplies, where she encountered an overseer and a fleeing slave. The overseer had asked Harriet to catch the slave, but the little girl refused, letting the slave get farther away. The overseer was so enraged that he threw a metal weight aimed at the running slave. Unfortunately for Harriet, the weight found its mark on her head instead, as she was in the way. The blow split her skull open, plunging her into unconsciousness. She endured two days without any kind of medical attention, and it's a miracle she made it out alive.

With this life-threatening injury came lots of seizures, severe headaches, and narcoleptic episodes that turned into a terrifying new normal for the young girl. These seizures would steal her consciousness and yet leave her strangely aware of the world around her. She would carry this unfortunate experience with her for the rest of her life. But, from the ashes of pain, something extraordinary sprung forth. Harriet began having vivid dreams where visions unfolded, whispers from the divine that ignited a passionate faith within her.

Though she couldn't read the Bible stories her mother shared with her and her siblings, the tales of deliverance in the Old Testament were treasured and kept deep within her soul. This newfound faith became her guiding light, and the story of Moses and the Israelites made her believe that she would someday lead her people to freedom.

The Moses of Her People

Harriet had changed her name from Araminta to Harriet in honor of her mother. In 1844, she married a free man from whom she took the last name *Tubman*. By the time her owner had passed away, there were whispers about the future of the enslaved people, including her family, and how they would be sold off and scattered further across the nation.

With this ache in her heart and being slightly weakened by her illness, a decision hardened in her soul: escape. And so, on the 17th of September 1849, Harriet made the move to escape slavery in Maryland with two of her brothers to Philadelphia, leaving behind her husband, John Tubman.

It wasn't a decision taken lightly, but she gathered the courage to do it. Before the mini family could go far, a bounty hunter's notice was plastered across the local paper, *Cambridge Democrat*, which promised a hefty reward of three hundred U.S. dollars for Harriet's capture. This new development sparked fear in the hearts of her two brothers, who had initially joined her quest for freedom. The boys wanted no trouble, so they decided to go back to Maryland and continue working as slaves.

But Harriet wouldn't be swayed. She had come too close to freedom to let it all go at this point. So, instead of surrendering, she bid farewell to her brothers, ensuring their safety, and then she ventured forth to Pennsylvania alone. At this time, the Underground Railroad symbolized for her a network of secret routes and safe houses, a path to freedom veiled in darkness. For nearly 90 miles, Harriet was on this trail, each step fueled by the burning desire for a new life.

While on the trail, Harriet must've poured her heart into her dear diary.

> *Dear Diary,*
>
> *Today, I started my journey north to freedom. It feels like a long, never-ending road, but it's a promise of a new life. Ninety miles seems impossible, but every step takes me closer to that dream that's kept me going all these years as a slave. The road doesn't look smooth, and memories of the plantation continue to plague my head. The heavyweight of slavery hanging on my skin like old scars. But with each mile, I feel less like a slave. It's like the ground itself wants me to be free, and I would not disappoint it.*
>
> *Sometimes, I fear that I might be caught, looking over my shoulders and listening for anything or anyone that might catch me. Every sound makes me jump, a reminder of the danger all around. But I have a reason to keep going, stronger than anything. I'm not just running away; I'm fighting for my freedom like a true soldier*

would. Like my mother had taught me. Every mile is closer to a place where I won't be a slave, where I can finally be free.

I think about all the people who tried to escape before me. They're like voices in my head, singing freedom songs. Every one of them who ended up being caught and taken back to slavery, or worse, killed. Their courage gives me strength, and even in the dark, their stories push me toward the light of a new day.

Ninety miles is a long way, but freedom is more than how far one can run, it's about one's true strength and the things that make them strong. No matter what the world ahead throws at me, I won't give up. There's a better life waiting for me on the other side, and I can't wait to have it.

Love,

Harriet

Finally, she crossed the border into Pennsylvania, a free state. Harriet felt decades of relief wash over her like a wave. Stepping onto free soil, she stared at her own hands, a sense of disbelief shimmering in her eyes. Was she truly free? "When I found I had crossed that line," she later recalled, "I looked at my hands to see if I was the same person. There was such a glory over everything; the sun came like gold through the trees and over the fields, and I felt like I was in Heaven." The shackles may have been physical, but the weight of bondage lifted in that moment. Harriet Tubman had finally tasted freedom, and she vowed not to rest until others did the same.

Harriet the Conductor

Harriet Tubman, like a modern-day Moses leading people out of slavery, became a superstar conductor on the Underground Railroad. While she served in this role, she risked everything to make 11 to 13 trips to the South, helping around 70 enslaved people escape to freedom. She was inspired by her own escape to pull others out of the shackles of slavery.

Map of the Underground Railroad route.

The legend was a master of disguise. Because of the bounty on her head, she would pretend to be a regular field hand working at safe houses or even fool people by reading a newspaper on a train. Sometimes, she would use costumes, dressing as a man or an old lady to throw people off her trail and go about her mission to free slaves in the South.

Smart and sneaky, Tubman preferred arranging the escape of slaves during the winter season so they could travel farther, being unseen during the long nights. Weekends were also her prime time for leaving because notices about runaway slaves wouldn't be printed in the newspapers until Monday. She carried a gun with her to protect herself and the people she helped. The gun also had other uses, as she would use it to threaten the scared and tired slaves to keep moving whenever they slowed down. She also carried with her some medicine to calm crying babies who might give them away as they moved.

Harriet studied the North Star and rivers that flowed north and learned how to use them as a compass for her travels. She had gotten a job in Philadelphia, and from there, she began to save money. She became acquaintances with some officials who could be bribed to look the other way every time she had some slaves on the run with her. She would use special songs, owl hoots, coded letters, and messengers to secretly talk to enslaved people and plan escapes.

In 1850, the Fugitive Slave Law was enacted. This was a law that stated slaves who escaped to the North could be caught and sent back to the South, even if they were free. This meant even Black people who were already free in the North were at risk. When she found out about this law, Harriet did not hesitate to change the Underground Railroad route she took to lead people all the way to Canada, where slavery wasn't allowed at all.

In December of 1851, Harriet led a group of 11 people who had escaped slavery on this new route to Canada. There's even some evidence that they stopped at the house of Frederick Douglass, a famous former slave who fought against slavery. A few years later, in 1858, Harriet met John Brown. This was a man who believed violence was the only way to end slavery, and Harriet agreed with his goal, even if she wasn't sure he was going about it the right way. He planned an attack on slave masters, and he asked Harriet, whom people now called "General Tubman," for help. She agreed to help, but sadly, the attack failed, and John Brown was captured and killed. To Harriet, the man would forever be the hero who laid down his life to fight for the freedom of people who had no hope.

> My dearest Diary,
>
> Freedom feels like a heavy bag filled with both joy and tears. The more people I help escape, the more sad I get because each victory reminds me of those still in chains, crying for freedom or worse accepting their fate as slaves forever.
>
> The death of dear John Brown breaks my heart. Not just me, but everyone who dreams of a world where all is fair, and slaves are free. His fight for freedom inspires us all. Now, with him gone, there's a hole that can't be filled.
>
> John had asked me to fight alongside him, to free more people. His words stirred something deep inside me. But even as I miss him, a part of me worries about what's next. Fighting for freedom is dangerous. Those who want slavery to stay will continue looking for ways to eliminate us.
>
> But now more than ever, I feel fire in my bones to fight for what's right. It's like a voice I can't shut out, telling me more people still need to be rescued. It

reminds me of how relieved I was when I became and how I vowed to bring this freedom to others. Standing here, scared but determined, I will never forget all the freedom fighters before me, they remind me this fight isn't mine alone, it's for everyone who wants a world without chains.

So, Diary, as I face what's to come, I hold onto the memory of those who died for freedom. We will keep walking, together, until freedom reaches all.

With love and hope,

Harriet

The Spy and the Civil Warrior

During the Civil War, Harriet wasn't afraid to put herself in danger for the Union cause. She had a vision that the war would lead to the end of slavery. She became a spy, using her knowledge of the land and the trust of enslaved people to gather crucial intel. She even led a daring raid up a river in South Carolina, freeing over 700 slaves and disrupting Confederate supplies. This brave act helped the Union win the battle and secure freedom for even more people. She also worked for the Union Army as a cook and a nurse, providing aid for soldiers who were suffering from dysentery and some infectious diseases.

Even after slavery ended, Harriet wouldn't rest. She became a champion for women's rights, standing alongside famous figures like Susan B. Anthony and Elizabeth Cady Stanton. She believed that everyone, regardless of race or gender, deserved equal rights and fought tirelessly to make that dream a reality. Helping people wasn't just a job for Tubman; it was a mission of love. Despite the danger and the price on her head, she never lost a single person she was helping. This bravery and success made her a legend, earning her the nickname "Moses."

Settling in her home in New York after the war, Harriet continued her work for freedom and equality. She worked hard to promote women's suffrage, traveling to different cities to speak about why women should be allowed to vote. She made it clear in her speeches that her sacrifices and those of the numerous women who fought for freedom should be considered as women's equality to men. With the help of friends, she even got a biography written about her amazing life. Her story continues to be an inspiration for people fighting for justice and equality today.

A True Legend

All over the world, people remember Harriet Tubman's bravery and how she fought to be free and helped others escape slavery, just like many people today fight against unfairness and for equal rights. For people who face racism and prejudice today, Harriet Tubman's story brings hope. She never stopped fighting for what was right, reminding us that the battle for equality isn't over. We still need to challenge racism and unfairness wherever we see them.

Harriet Tubman was also very adamant about women's equality. Just like she fought for their rights years ago, many women today have become activists seeking to break down barriers for women and allow them to have the same opportunities as men in everything they do.

Harriet Tubman's story teaches us about standing together and fighting for what's right. Movements like Black Lives Matter and protests against unfair treatment by police draw inspiration from her. She has walked her path, and her example shows us that when people work together, they can create a new system.

Famous Quotes

"If you hear the dogs, keep going. If you see the torches in the woods, keep going. If there's shouting after you, keep going. Don't ever stop. Keep going. If you want a taste of freedom, keep going."

- Harriet Tubman

"Twant me, 'twas the Lord. I always told him, 'I trust you. I don't know where to go or what to do, but I expect you to lead me,' and He always did."

- Harriet Tubman

Chapter 2: Unbowed Champion: The Nelson Mandela Journey

The winds of change were blowing in South Africa. For the first time, all races were allowed to participate in a democratic election. 1994 was a year of revolution. Power was handed over to the new African National Congress government without any bloodshed. The segregationist National Party was defeated at the ballot box. Nelson Rolihlahla Mandela, affectionately known by the South African people as "Tata," became the first democratically elected South African president in a free and fair society.

Nelson Mandela.
©copyright John Mathew Smith 2001.
https://commons.wikimedia.org/wiki/File:Nelson_Mandela_1994.jpg

As the title of Mandela's autobiography made clear, it was a "Long Walk to Freedom." The victory after years of struggle did not happen overnight. Having given his life to the liberation of the South African people, Nelson Mandela is commemorated with monuments throughout the nation, and his picture appears on the country's rand currency. Mandela embodies fighting for one's rights and rebuilding through unity.

The Early Years

Nelson Mandela grew up in the idyllic Eastern Village of Qunu. Rolihlahla was given the European name *Nelson* by his primary school teacher, Miss Mdingane. Mandela was the son of nobility. His father, Nkosi Mphakanyiswa Gadla Mandela, was the chief counselor to the King of the Thembu people. Mandela's mother, Nosekeni Fanny, was the third of four wives. Mandela was from a big family of 13 children. He was born in 1918, only five years after the Native Land Act of 1913 was passed, which reserved 93% of the country's land for the white minority. As Dutch colonialists expanded from the Cape, they dispossessed many of the Aboriginal cultures. Similarly, Mandela's family land was taken. After a dispute with a local magistrate, the colonial authorities stripped Mandela's father of his noble title and took his land and livestock, resulting in the family's move from Mvelo to Qunu.

Mandela inherited the revolutionary attitude of his father, who was not afraid to stand up to authority. The flames of his political consciousness were being stoked early in his life. Being from a powerful family with deep royal roots, Mandela was not brainwashed into the narratives of African inferiority. He learned about the valiance and brave exploits of his ancient ancestors passed down through unbroken chains of oral tradition. These seeds of a solid self-identity would sprout into the drive to fight for the dignity of Black people.

As a young cattle herder, Nelson Mandela would spend hours outside tending to the animals. He lived a typical farm-boy life of early mornings in the Eastern Cape breeze. Both of Mandela's parents were illiterate, and he was the first in his family to attend school. Mandela matriculated at Wesleyan Secondary School. He then went on to study for a Bachelor of Arts degree at Fort Hare. He did not complete the qualification. The fight against injustice took priority over his studies, so he got kicked out for organizing a student protest. He returned to Fort Hare to graduate in 1943 after studying for a BA at the University of South Africa.

The King of the Thembu people, Jongintaba Dalindyebo, was furious when he found out about Mandela getting kicked out of college. The king planned to arrange marriages for Nelson Mandela and his cousin, Justice, but the two opted to explore the city life of Johannesburg. Mandela also went on to study an LLB at the University of Witwatersrand, but with his focus elsewhere, he was not able to complete the qualification. He resumed his studies well into his political career at the University of London after going to the UK to garner support for the South African struggle. In 1989, Mandela finally completed his LLB while finishing the last stretch of his 27-year prison sentence.

The seeds for revolution were already planted in Mandela by the ancestral teachings he gained from his father at an early age. Through his pursuit of education, he was awakened to the injustices of the world around him, allowing him to grow into his political identity. As his political consciousness expanded, he started organizing with fellow students against the discriminatory policies of the apartheid government. Mandela's early life laid the foundation for the bulk of his political career as a member of the liberating party, the African National Congress (or the ANC). Without the experiences of his youth, he likely would not have grown into the icon he later became.

Struggle Against Apartheid

Apartheid is an Afrikaans word that means "separateness." It was a system of laws and social norms that grouped races into a hierarchy. Whites or Europeans were on the top, followed by Indians, then Coloreds or people of mixed origins, and lastly, Black Africans. It was illegal for the groups to interact socially. They lived in different areas with varying levels of access to resources based on their racial identity. They couldn't use the same toilets, benches, or drinking fountains. The lines between races were chillingly clear, and the consequences of transgressing the segregation laws were brutal.

A nurse in apartheid reported that she had mixed up the sheets for the white people and Black people in the hospital. Since they could not risk sending the sheets the Black people may have contaminated to the white section, the head nurse insisted that the sheets needed to be discarded. In the same hospital, a Black woman had a child with a colored man. Years later, the mother and the daughter ended up sick. The Black mother and colored daughter were served different food because different races couldn't eat the same. The mother was heartbroken and outraged, failing to understand how the child she had given birth to now deserved different food than she did.

The folly of these laws resulted in ridiculous tests to determine racial identity. One of these assessments was the "Pencil Test," where a pencil was put into an individual's hair to see if it stuck in order to determine if the texture indicated whiteness or Blackness. The apartheid system not only socially and economically separated people, but it did so with violence. People were forcibly moved out of their homes. Black people needed passes to be in white neighborhoods or risk getting arrested and beaten. Every aspect of public life was racially segregated, including recreational areas and transport.

These conditions and unfair treatment of the Black masses along racial lines created a pressure cooker where uprisings were inevitable. Throughout the struggle, various groups took up the mantle of resistance, including the SACP, AZAPO, PAC, IFP, and the group Mandela joined, which would eventually become the ruling party, the ANC. These organizations mobilized the masses to revolt against the totalitarian and racist government of the day. Many of them were declared terrorist groups, with their leaders being arrested for treason and other crimes against the state. These groups would, at different times, take up both violent and non-violent strategies.

Mandela's political legs began running in 1942 before he finally joined the ANC. When he joined the organization in 1944 as a young activist, he was filled with the explosive energy that the revolution needed. Early after joining the ANC, Mandela helped found the ANC Youth League, which was a wing that mobilized young people in the struggle against apartheid. He formulated the Program for Action, which was used to get the masses involved.

In 1952, Nelson Mandela was given a key role as the Volunteer-in-Chief of the Defiance Campaign. The Campaign of Defiance against Unjust Laws was a mass action of civil disobedience created by the ANC and the South African Indian Congress. The nonviolent movement organized people to break racist laws by entering segregated spaces or staying out after curfew without passes. Due to its peaceful nature of nonviolently disobeying oppressive laws, the movement garnered widespread support.

Nelson Mandela attended the All-in-Africa Conference days before being tried for treason in 1956. The conference concluded with a resolution stating that Mandela was to write a letter to Prime Minister Verwoerd demanding a non-racial constitution that benefited all South Africans. Between March 29 and March 30, Mandela went underground to begin planning for the strike, but it was canceled because the state security of the apartheid government kicked into overdrive to prevent the mass movement. A police swoop that resulted in the arrest of 28 people, including Mandela, did not yield fruitful outcomes for the apartheid regime. All of the accused in the Treason Trial in 1956 were acquitted.

One of the most devasting tragedies in South African history occurred in Sharpeville in 1961. 69 unarmed people were killed by police firing live rounds into a crowd who were protesting pass laws. This increased the sentiment for violent resistance amongst the people. In 1961, uMkhonto we Sizwe was established. This was the military wing of the ANC resistance movement, whose name is translated in English as "The Spear of the Nation." The resistance tactics of explosions brought more heat onto the revolutionary movements pushing for change.

This increasing pressure from the government meant that Nelson Mandela had to move stealthily. He took on the alias of David Motsamayi in January 1962. Mandela used this new identity to travel to England and around Africa. He got military training in Morocco and Ethiopia. Many fighters in the struggle also trained in Russia and Cuba due to the socialist leanings of liberation movements like the ANC. Mandela returned to South Africa in August 1962. He was stopped at a roadblock where he was identified, which ended up with him getting a five-year prison sentence. This started a chain of events that led to him getting locked up for 27 years.

Robben Island

On October 9, 1963, the most impactful trial in South African history commenced. Mandela and ten other accused stood trial. Mandela made his popular "Speech on the Dock" in 1964 while addressing the court.

Staring down the threat of the death penalty, Mandela uttered the immortal words:

"I have cherished the ideal of a democratic and free society in which all persons live together in harmony and with equal opportunities. It is

an ideal that I hope to live for and to achieve. But if needs be, it is an ideal for which I am prepared to die."

Nelson Mandela, Walter Sisulu, Govan Mbeki, Denis Goldberg, Raymond Mhlaba, Elias Motsoaledi, Andrew Mlangeni, and Ahmed Kathrada were all sentenced the next day. Today, Robben Island is a historic tourist destination, but back then, it was a feared prison for political criminals. Mandela's decades of reflection in prison helped him develop a unique outlook on the ongoing struggle. His communications were limited, so he was largely cut off from the outside world but was able to receive bits and pieces of information. Mandela wrote hundreds of letters while in prison, some of which have been published.

During his time in prison, his wife, Winnie Mandela, was constantly harassed by the apartheid government. On different occasions, she was detained, beaten, and dragged from her home. She rose as the face of the struggle and represented the vision of Nelson Mandela. She was cold to the apartheid regime and had no mercy in her words or actions against them. She garnered harsh criticism for her militancy. She stood by Mandela throughout his prison time, and he often wrote to her about the deeper personal issues he was experiencing behind the concrete walls. Mandela confided in her how prison gave him time to reflect on himself and the world.

Mandela developed close relationships with his Afrikaner prison guards. He learned to speak their language fluently because he asserted that using someone's mother tongue allows you to speak to their soul. He learned a lot about the Afrikaner point of view, and he also taught them about the Black struggle in South Africa. This gave him the tools he needed to navigate the negotiation process of the transition into an inclusive democracy.

Even in prison, Nelson Mandela's commitment to the people stood solid. When offered conditional release by the government, Mandela rejected it, stating that there was no separation between his freedom and the freedom of his people. His daughter, Zindziswa, read the rejection letter to a cheering crowd in Jabulani stadium. In 1990, Mandela was released after the ANC and PAC were unbanned. This began the process of the transition into a non-racial government.

Freedom, Non-Violence, and Reconciliation

Nelson Mandela's story is incomplete without a mention of his former wife, the late Winnie Mandela. South Africans consider her the mother of the nation. While Nelson Mandela was locked up, Winnie kept the spirit of revolution and the struggle against the apartheid regime alive. Winnie's methods were controversial because of the ultra-militant stance she took against the oppressive power. Some of the most bone-chilling descriptions of the struggle come from stories of Winnie's forces burning apartheid informants alive in the townships.

Winnie Mandela.
John Mathew Smith & www.celebrity-photos.com from Laurel, Maryland, USA, CC BY-SA 2.0 <https://creativecommons.org/licenses/by-sa/2.0>, via Wikimedia Commons. https://commons.wikimedia.org/wiki/File:Winnie_Mandela_2.jpg

Nelson Mandela was freed after 27 years in prison to a massive parade welcoming home the struggle hero in 1990, with Winnie Mandela at his side. They would get divorced shortly after his release from prison. Some believe it was due to ideological differences, with Winnie demanding justice while Mandela was building the roads to forgiveness. In the next election, he became the first president of the new South Africa.

The atrocities of apartheid are unimaginable. Many Black people understandably cried out for vengeance on their former oppressors as Nelson Mandela began governing the country. Ardent supporters of Nelson Mandela did not fully understand the route he was taking with his reconciliation stance. People expected Mandela to pursue punitive vengeance, especially after having spent 27 years in prison as a direct result of the prior apartheid system. They cried out to Mandela, begging him to seek brutal justice for the unspeakable torture they had suffered under the apartheid regime.

The Truth and Reconciliation Commission was created by Nelson Mandela and chaired by Bishop Desmond Tutu. The controversial commission was established to help the country heal from the wounds of apartheid and move forward as a new democratic nation. The TRC allowed the victims of human rights violations under the previous regime to come forward and tell their stories, and amnesty would be granted to the perpetrators of the crimes who took their actions to fulfill a political agenda. The TRC's Black critics said that there was no justice in the process, and the white critics emphasized that these stories could aggravate racial tensions. Further, controversy would rise as the TRC was set up voluntarily, meaning that perpetrators and victims were not forced to show up. PW Botha, a former state president, refused to attend the proceedings, exposing the flaws in the process.

Although the TRC wasn't perfect, it steered the country away from the brink of violent destruction. It was the first layer in establishing the new inclusive South Africa. Mandela's emphasis on forgiveness as someone who greatly suffered under apartheid rule inspired the Black masses to embody humanity to their former oppressors. The focus on reconciliation under Mandela allowed South Africa to have an economic boom as the country opened to international investment. His non-violent legacy and commitment to unity followed the heroic leader throughout his life. Although the processes of the TRC may have been flawed, the spirit of reconciliation helped paint the picture of South Africa's multiracial future.

Madiba Magic

Madiba is the name of Nelson Mandela's clan. It is a tradition in South Africa to show people respect by calling them by their clan name because they are representing them well. It is a way to pay homage to one's ancestors. Madiba Magic is used to describe Mandela's unique ability to charm crowds and get the most unlikely people to get along. The general feeling of unity he was able to create in a country that had just emerged from violent division seemed almost supernatural.

This magnetic draw may have contributed to why the struggle hero got international admiration as a Nobel Peace Prize winner. Mandela could make everyone feel comfortable while unapologetically asserting his point of view. His calls for a united South Africa were embodied in his actions, and his commitment to the continued upliftment of Black people never faltered until his death.

Today, Mandela is celebrated worldwide.

Madiba Magic was his ability to make people believe the vision of a reconciled South Africa that builds prosperity and equality for all. Wherever Mandela went, people would flock to him, and he would often prevent his security guards from limiting their access too much. Mandela was truly the people's president, and his charisma was fully on display in any room he entered. His distinctive speech pattern and flamboyant patterned shirts will forever be remembered.

The Battle against HIV/AIDS in South Africa

Mandela's early efforts against the budding epidemic of HIV in South Africa were non-existent. The ANC government largely ignored this public health crisis. Thabo Mbeki, who took the presidency after Nelson Mandela, stated that HIV did not cause AIDS and that the illness was not fatal. His denialism set the country back years in fighting the disease.

However, later, Nelson Mandela realized his mistake as the HIV/AIDS epidemic spiraled out of control. In 2003, he set up the Nelson Mandela Foundation, which was created to combat HIV. Under the 46664 brand, which was his prison number on Robben Island, Mandela began fundraising efforts to provide education about the virus. He emphasized that people needed to talk about the disease to remove the stigma so that individuals could get the help they needed. In 2005, his son, Makgatho, tragically died of AIDS. Mandela addressed the press, admitting his shortcomings and emphasizing the need for measures to be taken to combat the disease.

Tata's Legacy

Mandela died of old age at home in 2013. Today, South Africans face many challenges as a young democracy. The undercurrents of racial tension still haunt the nation. Poverty, inequality, and government corruption plague the country. However, Nelson Mandela is still upheld as a shining light to guide the country out of the darkness. Sentiments in modern South Africa are shifting from reconciliation to justice among large sections of the population. Many believe that the revolution that Mandela started is incomplete because of the large economic inequality that still exists. However, some believe that uplifting the memory of Mandela can reawaken the drive to work together to address the problems of South Africa. In an increasingly divided world where everyone retreats into ideological bubbles, Mandela's model of extending an olive branch to find common ground may be more relevant now than it was in his lifetime.

Mandela was not only a leader and a freedom fighter, but the legacy of his philanthropic activities also stands tall. The Nelson Mandela Children's Fund, The Nelson Mandela Foundation, and The Mandela Rhodes Foundation all still function to help those in need and provide opportunities to the underprivileged. His lifelong battle against racism and inequality, as well as his commitment to reconciliation, has etched Nelson Mandela as an iconic symbol for the world to emulate.

Chapter 3: The Soaring Intellect: Katherine Johnson's Mathematical Mastery

Katherine Johnson's fascination with numbers was visible from an early age. Little did she know that her love for math would shape the course of history. As a mathematician and rocket scientist, Katherine dedicated her life to studying gravity and motion in space. Her brilliance and dedication were unmatched, which led her to become an integral part of the National Aeronautics and Space Administration (NASA). It was Katherine's calculations that paved the way for some of NASA's most famous missions, including John Glenn's historic orbit of Earth in 1962.

Katherine Johnson.
https://commons.wikimedia.org/wiki/File:Katherine_Johnson_1983.jpg

What makes Katherine's achievements even more remarkable is that she accomplished all of this without the help of modern computers. In a time when technology was still in its early stages, Katherine acted as a literal human computer at NASA. She crunched numbers better than the computers of the time and ensured each mission was a success. Her contributions were so invaluable that even when NASA began using computers, they turned to Katherine to double-check their work.

However, was it always so easy for her? Katherine's road to success was anything but straightforward. She had to go through a series of challenges while facing discrimination and skepticism along the way. She was a woman and a woman of color at that, so it was anything but simple for her to get where she did and achieve what she did. Despite these hurdles, Katherine was fueled by her unwavering determination and thirst for knowledge.

This is Katherine Johnson's story: a tale full of tough challenges, never giving up, and always striving to do her best. It's a story that shows no matter who you are or where you come from. You can achieve amazing things if you keep pushing forward. From her beginnings to her amazing work at NASA, Katherine showed the world that anything is possible with determination and hard work. She broke down barriers, showed that anyone can do great things, and inspired people everywhere to believe in themselves and chase their dreams.

Early Life

Born in 1918 in White Sulphur Springs, West Virginia, Katherine was the youngest of four children born to Joshua and Joylette Coleman. Even from a young age, it was clear that Katherine possessed a unique talent for mathematics, and she was always happy to help her siblings as they tackled homework together around the family table. Growing up in a time when racial segregation was common, Katherine's parents understood the importance of education and tried to find opportunities for their children beyond the limitations imposed by their segregated community.

They sent Katherine and her siblings to a school in Institute, West Virginia, located on the campus of West Virginia State College. At West Virginia State College, Katherine shone brightly. She excelled in her studies and, in fact, skipped several grades and graduated from high school at just the age of 14. She wasted no time in pursuing higher education and enrolled at West Virginia State College, a Historically Black College, where she found a supportive community among her peers.

At West Virginia State College, Katherine's potential caught the eye of two influential mentors who would shape her future. Angie Turner King, a mathematician and scientist, recognized Katherine's brilliance and took her under her wing. Additionally, William Schieffelin Claytor, the third African American to receive a doctoral degree in mathematics, saw Katherine's talent and provided her with advanced math classes to further hone her skills.

Despite societal expectations that limited career options for women, Katherine graduated summa cum laude from West Virginia State College in 1937 with dual degrees in mathematics and French. Initially, she could only consider a career in nursing or teaching, and therefore, she started her professional journey as a teacher at a public school in Marion, Virginia.

Katherine Johnson's upbringing was marked by an awareness of racism, but it wasn't until she entered the workforce that she encountered its harsh realities firsthand. Her first job as a teacher required her to travel to Virginia, where racial tensions were particularly high. Despite her mother's warnings about the challenging environment, Katherine remained undeterred, defiantly declaring, "Well, tell them I'm coming."

However, fate had bigger plans in store for Katherine. In 1938, a landmark Supreme Court case, Missouri ex rel. Lloyd Gaines v. Canada ruled that states providing higher education options to white students must also extend the same opportunities to African American students. This ruling paved the way for West Virginia State College's president, John Davis, to recommend Katherine and two male African-American students for enrollment in the graduate program at West Virginia University, the state's white school.

Katherine's acceptance into the graduate program at West Virginia University marked a historic milestone, as she was one of the first African American students to integrate into the program. However, after a year, Katherine made the difficult decision to leave the program to focus on her family with her first husband, James Goble. Despite this setback, Katherine's journey was far from over. Her early life was just the beginning of a remarkable trajectory that would lead her to become one of the most influential figures in space exploration history.

Family, Career, and Space Exploration

Katherine Johnson's life was not just about groundbreaking math and space missions. It was also about family, sacrifice, and unwavering dedication. After marrying her husband, James, they welcomed three baby girls into their family: Constance, Joylette, and Katherine. Despite her demanding career, Katherine always put her family first. She was not only a brilliant mathematician but also a loving mother who taught her daughters valuable skills like sewing, all while using her mathematical talents to help others.

In addition to her regular job, Katherine dedicated her spare time to tutoring others in math, never asking for anything in return. Her kindness and generosity knew no bounds. When James fell ill, Katherine became his primary caregiver, devoting herself to his care until his passing in 1956. Despite facing personal loss, Katherine remained resilient and determined to forge ahead.

In 1959, Katherine found love again and married James Johnson. Little did she know that this union would coincide with a pivotal moment in her career. During a family gathering, a relative mentioned job opportunities for math specialists at NASA's Langley Research Center in Hampton, Virginia. The National Advisory Committee for Aeronautics (NACA) was in search of women with a strong background in mathematics to join their team. These women were given the title of "computers" because they were responsible for carrying out complex calculations for the male engineers employed at NACA. Katherine herself famously remarked that during that time, "the computer wore a skirt."

Russia and the United States were engaged in a fierce Cold War rivalry at this time, with both countries vying to create cutting-edge aircraft for use in the defense of their respective countries. Thus, the work being done by NACA's computers was crucial at that particular time. NACA was segregated even though federal law forbade discrimination in government employment. The agency kept the "White" and "Black" computer divisions apart. Surprisingly, Black computer candidates had to meet stricter recruiting standards than their white counterparts. White candidates were not held to the same academic standards as Black applicants, who had to have college degrees and high GPAs. Because of this disparity, the engineers frequently chose to work with the Black "computers" that were more capable.

Undeterred by the challenges posed by segregation, Katherine Johnson decided to pursue the opportunity at NACA. She drove to the NACA facility and requested an application, determined to showcase her abilities and secure a position. Despite the initial hurdles, Katherine's perseverance paid off when one year later, NACA offered her a job. Katherine Johnson's first day at NACA was nothing short of extraordinary. Katherine was astounded to see so many Black women working in professional settings, each with their own desks and computers.

It was a rare and empowering moment to see a space where women of color were not only present but also thriving in their roles.

"I stood there astounded . . . Back then, a room filled with so many professional [Black] women was a rare sight . . . not one of them was a teacher or a nurse . . . nor were any of them domestics."

Katherine Johnson at NASA.

When she joined NASA, she wasn't the only African American woman there. Dozens of women like her worked at Langley as human computers, tackling incredibly complex calculations for various projects in the space race. While the job paid better than many other options available to educated women at the time, around $2,000 per year, they still faced discrimination.

At the research lab, segregation was a harsh reality. African American women were forced to work in separate "colored" workspaces, even though they were doing the exact same work as their white counterparts. They were located a mile away from the other women and had to endure facilities without even basic amenities like toilets. In contrast, the white women were provided with accommodation nearby, while Katherine and her colleagues had to make their own arrangements.

Just two weeks into her new job, Katherine's talents were quickly recognized by her superiors. An engineer sought assistance from the Black computers' office, and Katherine was singled out by her boss as one of the brightest minds among them. She accompanied the engineer into an office filled with white men and was tasked with reviewing a set of calculations. With her keen eye for detail, she immediately identified an error and confidently brought it to the attention of the team leader. Despite the initial embarrassment, the team leader acknowledged Katherine's correction and recognized her exceptional analytical abilities.

Katherine's proactive approach quickly made her valuable to the engineering team. While most computers were rotated from project to project, Katherine's expertise and dedication ensured that she remained an integral part of their team. Her contributions were highly valued, and her presence was deemed indispensable to the success of their missions.

Katherine's brilliance could not be ignored for long. Her calculations and dedication to accuracy earned her a stellar reputation at NASA. She played an essential role in shaping the possibilities of aeronautics during that era, co-writing scientific papers and even helping to write NASA's first textbook on space.

Despite the challenges of working in a segregated environment, Katherine found ways to fight against the blatant discrimination happening at NASA. She refused to adhere to the segregated bathroom regulations and asserted her rights to use whichever facilities she deemed appropriate. Similarly, she avoided eating in the segregated cafeteria, choosing instead to assert her autonomy and dignity in her own way.

During breaks, Katherine managed to connect with her white male colleagues by engaging in card games and discussions about aviation magazines. Despite the racial divide, Katherine sought common ground with her coworkers. In her quest for equality and recognition, Katherine successfully demanded to be included in high-level briefings and participate in the important decision-making processes within the organization.

While people rightly celebrate the achievements of the white men who landed on the moon, they often forget about the countless women, particularly African Americans, who played vital roles behind the scenes. Despite facing immense challenges during the height of segregation, these women excelled in their jobs, assisting NASA in trajectory calculations, analyzing data from wind resistance tests, and solving the complex problems involved in spacecraft re-entering Earth's atmosphere safely. Their contributions were instrumental in the success of NASA's missions, yet their stories have often been overlooked or marginalized in the broader narrative of space exploration.

As the Cold War escalated and the space race intensified, NACA evolved into the National Aeronautics and Space Administration (NASA) with a renewed mission to put Americans into space. Katherine threw herself into her work with even greater determination. In 1961, Katherine's expertise was put to the test when she calculated the trajectory for Alan Shepard, the first American in space. Without her calculations, the mission would not have been a success.

Astronaut John Glenn was poised to make history as the first American to orbit the Earth. NASA, relying on a series of mechanical computers to calculate this trajectory, faced the challenge of ensuring the accuracy and reliability of their calculations. Despite the availability of these new computing machines, which were not always dependable, John Glenn had unwavering confidence in Katherine Johnson's mathematical abilities.

Upon reviewing the mission plan, John Glenn made a specific request to NASA: he insisted that if "the girl" said the math was correct, he was ready to go on the historic journey. The "girl" in question was none other than Katherine Johnson. Faced with the monumental task of calculating the trajectory by hand, Katherine spent nearly two entire days crunching the numbers. Her efforts paid off when, on February 20, 1962, John Glenn successfully completed three orbits around the planet and safely returned to Earth, with Katherine's calculations proving to be accurate and reliable.

Despite the initial anonymity surrounding her role in the project, Katherine's contributions eventually got attention from the Black press, and she was thus celebrated as a mother, a wife, and a career woman whose achievements were above traditional gender and racial boundaries.

When President Kennedy issued the challenge for NASA to land a spacecraft on the moon, Katherine Johnson again played a key role in the mission. She spent incredible effort and time devising the complex calculations required to launch a spacecraft into the moon's orbit and orchestrate the intricate rendezvous between orbiting and lunar-landing craft.

In July 1969, as the United States achieved the historic feat of landing on the moon, Katherine found herself in a surprising location — not at home or in the office, but attending a college reunion. Unbeknownst to many in attendance, Katherine had completed her calculations for the moon landing well in advance. As her former classmates gathered around a hotel television to witness Neil Armstrong's historic steps on the lunar surface, few realized Katherine's critical role in making that moment possible.

Upon her return from the reunion, Katherine wasted no time in shifting her focus to new horizons. Already immersed in her next project, she directed her formidable intellect toward calculating the intricate trajectories required for sending a person to Mars.

Katherine's contributions didn't end there. In 1970, the Apollo 13 mission faced a catastrophic oxygen tank explosion. This catastrophic event jeopardized the lives of the three astronauts on board — Jim Lovell, Fred Haise, and Jack Swigert — and threatened the success of the mission.

In the aftermath of the explosion, NASA's Mission Control had to devise a plan to safely bring the astronauts back to Earth. Katherine Johnson, renowned for her expertise in trajectory analysis and orbital mechanics, was called upon to assist in the complex calculations required for the mission's reentry trajectory.

Katherine's calculations were instrumental in determining the precise trajectory adjustments needed to guide the spacecraft safely back to Earth amid the unprecedented challenges posed by the damaged service module. Her swift and accurate computations provided critical guidance to the flight controllers and astronauts, enabling them to navigate through space and execute the necessary maneuvers to ensure a successful reentry into Earth's atmosphere.

Awards and Honors

After dedicating more than 30 years of her life to NASA, Katherine Johnson retired from the agency in 1986. Throughout her tenure, she provided invaluable expertise for the official Space Shuttle program and conducted crucial research on human spaceflight, including studies on the feasibility of missions to Mars. Despite facing countless cases of racism within the agency, her contributions were undeniable.

In recognition of her remarkable achievements, NASA honored Katherine by naming a building after her: The Katherine G. Johnson Computational Research Facility. It is located on the grounds of NASA's campus in Hampton, Virginia.

Katherine's influence extended beyond the realm of aerospace engineering. Her story inspired toy brands like Barbie and Lego to create figures in her likeness, aimed at encouraging children, especially girls, to pursue interests in science, technology, engineering, and mathematics (STEM).

In 2015, President Barack Obama awarded Katherine Johnson the highest civilian honor in the United States: the Presidential Medal of Freedom. This prestigious accolade recognized her groundbreaking contributions to science and her tireless advocacy for equality and inclusion in STEM fields.

Katherine receiving the Presidential Medal of Freedom from President Obama.

The following year, Katherine's remarkable story reached a wider audience with the release of the Hollywood movie, "Hidden Figures." The film depicted the untold story of Katherine and other African-American women mathematicians who played pivotal roles at NASA during the Space Race. Despite her monumental achievements, Katherine remained humble about her contributions to science, embodying grace and humility throughout her life.

Even in her retirement, Katherine continued to make a difference in her community. She remained an active member of her local church choir for over 50 years. Her dedication to her faith and work exemplified her unwavering commitment to serving others and positively impacting the world. She passed away in 2020 at the age of 101 after living a full, beautiful, and inspiring life.

More than 75 years after leaving graduate school, Katherine's contributions to the field of astrophysics were finally recognized with the conferral of an honorary doctorate degree by West Virginia University.

This prestigious honor was bestowed upon Katherine in acknowledgment of her unparalleled accomplishments and significant leadership in the field.

In 2021, NASA made a special announcement that warmed hearts all over: they named a spacecraft after Katherine Johnson. The spacecraft was called the S.S. Katherine Johnson and was part of a mission called NG-15 Cygnus. This mission was about the delivery of supplies and equipment to astronauts living on the International Space Station (ISS).

Katherine Johnson's legacy lives on as an inspiration to countless individuals, proving that determination, intellect, and perseverance can overcome even the greatest of obstacles. Her pioneering spirit continues to inspire future generations to reach for the stars and pursue their dreams no matter the odds.

Chapter 4: Renaissance of Rhythm: Duke Ellington's Jazz Innovations

It was a time when neon signs were fairly new, the rise in the use of automobiles was generating a smoky haze on the streets, and cutting-edge technology like radios and telephones was becoming common. The Harlem Renaissance, a cultural revolution that would one day lead to the game-changing civil rights movement of the 1950s, was rapidly gaining momentum. It ushered in the Jazz Age when the brassy notes of trumpets and the harmonic sounds of saxophones could be heard every night in many parts of the country.

Duke Ellington.
https://commons.wikimedia.org/wiki/File:Duke_Ellington_1964.jpg

During this progressive time for African Americans, a young boy in his early 20s often played the piano at low-key house parties, hoping to get a break in the burgeoning jazz scene, but his meager earnings prompted him to close up shop and return home. He was the legendary jazz musician Duke Ellington, and this chapter traces his inspirational journey from his humble beginnings, many failures, and eventual triumphs that changed the fortunes of the Black community forever.

His Early Life

Duke Ellington's birth name was Edward Kennedy Ellington, and he was named after the middle names of his parents, James Edward Ellington and Daisy Kennedy Ellington. He was born on April 29, 1899, in Washington, D.C. Thanks to his parents, who were professional pianists, he was exposed to music from an early age. They nurtured his natural affinity for the art, providing him with piano lessons at the tender age of seven.

Duke was raised in a middle-class environment, but his parents weren't so fortunate. James Edward grew up in Lincolnton, North Carolina, a rural town back in the 1880s. He was a part of the Great Migration when his family moved to Washington, D.C., a few years after his birth. Daisy Kennedy's parents were once slaves, and she faced many hardships as a child. Nevertheless, James and Daisy were Duke's main source of motivation for his spectacular musical career ahead.

There is an interesting story behind his name change from Edward to Duke. His family was proud of their racial and cultural heritage, but the segregation laws (Jim Crow laws) of that time were harsh against African Americans. Daisy Kennedy wasn't one to take the injustice lying down. She mingled with the dignified women in her neighborhood, taking Edward along with her.

Eventually, their manners and style rubbed off on Edward. His friends noticed his elevated personality and refined dressing sense, which is why they began calling him "Duke." The name stuck throughout his life and career.

His Early Career

As a child, Duke Ellington loved visual arts, but later in life, his passion for music took over and made him one of the most recognizable faces of his era. As a young musician, he was talented as both a pianist and a composer, quickly earning recognition for his innovative style and charismatic performances.

In the 1910s, Ellington began performing in local bands around Washington, D.C., but he wasn't earning much, so he had to work odd jobs. It was during his stint as a soda jerk at the Poodle Dog Café that he created his first original composition, called "Soda Fountain Rag." He presented it in so many different and unique ways that people thought he was playing different compositions. It didn't take long for him to become the most sought-after pianist in his neighborhood and beyond.

In his late teens, Duke experienced many ups and downs in his musical journey. He became a part of several jazz bands before launching his first musical group, "The Duke's Serenaders," in 1917. His band instruments initially included a string bass, a trumpet, and a banjo. Later, in 1919, the drummer, Sunny Greer, who would go on to become a legendary musician in his own right, joined The Duke's Serenaders.

Ellington's more severe challenges and major successes came after 1919 when he decided to move with his band to New York City, where the evolving jazz scene was gradually sweeping people off their feet. In Harlem, he socialized with many famous artists like Noble Sissle and Willie Smith (The Lion), but he wasn't able to make a mark in the bustling cultural nightlife of the neighborhood.

Disheartened and depressed, he took his ensemble back to Washington. It was there that his fortunes changed for the better. His group changed its name to "Elmer Snowden and his Black Sox Orchestra" (after the banjo player), and they bagged several gigs over the years. In 1923, when jazz music was scaling new heights, they changed their name again to "The Washingtonians" and began making waves in the city.

By the mid-1920s, Ellington and his band had achieved national acclaim, securing a residency at the legendary Cotton Club in Harlem. It was here that Ellington's music reached a wider audience, as radio broadcasts brought his innovative sound into homes across America. Throughout the decade, Ellington continued to push the boundaries of jazz, experimenting with new forms and styles while remaining true to his roots.

The early years of Duke Ellington's career laid the foundation for his later achievements as a composer, bandleader, and cultural icon. His pioneering spirit, boundless creativity, and unwavering dedication to his craft would propel him to become one of the most influential figures in the history of American music.

The Cotton Club Tales

The Cotton Club was a prestigious nightclub in the heart of Harlem. Established in 1923 during the Prohibition era, it quickly became one of the most renowned entertainment venues in the United States. Although its entertainment lineup was predominantly African American, its clientele was restricted to white and affluent Americans.

Over the years, the Cotton Club's stage featured some of the most iconic musicians, dancers, and entertainers of the era, from Cab Calloway to Lena Horne. It didn't take long for Duke Ellington to become a part of their prestigious lineup. His association arose from his growing reputation as a bandleader and composer, but it also involved a bit of luck.

The Cotton Club in the 1930s, New York.
https://commons.wikimedia.org/wiki/File:Cotton_Club_1930.jpg

It so happened that Irving Mills, one of the most reputable agent-publishers of that age, secured a contract with Ellington in 1926 when he was still not too well-known. He helped him record on almost every famous label, from Brunswick to Columbia. Then, one fine day in September 1927, King Oliver, a regular house band lead at the Cotton Club, canceled their commitment for unknown reasons. Mills jumped on the opportunity and secured an audition spot at the club for Ellington. This is probably where his big band jazz originated.

One of the residency requirements was that Ellington increase his six-piece group to eleven. Instead of assigning a strict composition structure, he encouraged his band members to come up with their own melodies and interpretations of his compositions. Needless to say, the group easily cracked the audition to bag a residency as the house band.

The Cotton Club provided a platform for Ellington to showcase his unique style of jazz, which blended elements of blues, swing, and orchestral music, setting him apart from other bandleaders of the time. His performances were met with critical acclaim, and he quickly became one of the club's star attractions. Thanks to the club's regular radio broadcasts, his talent was appreciated throughout the country.

One of the notable aspects of Ellington's tenure at the Cotton Club was his ability to tailor the music to suit the club's clientele and the demands of the venue. He composed and arranged music specifically for the shows. His compositions, such as "Mood Indigo," "It Don't Mean a Thing (If It Ain't Got That Swing)," and "Sophisticated Lady," which would go on to become classics, were created and performed as the Cotton Club's house band.

Ellington's fame, however, didn't make him immune to the challenges faced by the Black community during his era. He and his band had to endure racial segregation and exploitation by the club's owners. They were not allowed to mingle with the white patrons or even enter the club through the front door.

However, Ellington's talent and charisma would one day transcend these barriers, for he would use his popularity to challenge racial segregation and pave the way toward greater acceptance and recognition of African-American artists in mainstream entertainment.

Across America and Europe

Duke Ellington's tours across America and Europe were pivotal moments in his career, showcasing his immense talent and spreading the gospel of jazz to audiences around the world. In the United States, after making a long-standing mark in Harlem, he and his orchestra embarked on numerous tours, crisscrossing the country from coast to coast. These tours took them to cities big and small, from the jazz hotbed of Chicago to where the genre was born – New Orleans.

One of the challenges Ellington faced during these tours was navigating the racial segregation that ran rampant in many parts of the country. Hotels, restaurants, and concert venues enforced strict segregation laws, forcing him to endure the indignity of separate accommodations and facilities. Regardless of these obstacles, he remained undeterred, focusing on his music and using it as a tool for social change.

In the spring of 1933, Ellington and his orchestra set sail for Europe, embarking on a journey that would captivate audiences and leave an indelible mark on the continent's music scene. Their tour took them to some of Europe's most prestigious venues, from the grand concert halls of Paris to the elegant ballrooms of London. Everywhere they went, they were met with enthusiasm and admiration since many European audiences had simply heard about jazz, not actually listened to it.

In Paris, their performances at venues like the Moulin Rouge and the Palais de Chaillot drew crowds of music lovers and cultural elites alike, earning them rave reviews in the French press. But, it was in London where Ellington truly made his mark. Their residency at the famous Trocadero Club became the talk of the town, with crowds lining up around the block to catch a glimpse of Duke in action. From royalty and celebrities to the common people, everyone wanted to be a part of the Ellington experience.

Throughout their tour, Ellington and his orchestra served as cultural ambassadors, bridging the gap between America and Europe through the universal language of music. In the years that followed, Duke would return to Europe many times, but it was that first tour in 1933 that laid the foundation for his enduring legacy as a pioneer of American music.

One of the highlights of Ellington's European tours was his historic performance at the Newport Jazz Festival in 1956. The concert, which featured a spectacular rendition of "Diminuendo and Crescendo in Blue" with saxophonist Paul Gonsalves, is widely regarded as one of the greatest moments in jazz history. It opened the next chapter in his life — his collaborations with other greats of his era.

His Collaborations with Other Jazz Legends

When it comes to jazz legends, Duke Ellington may be the best-known of the lot, but he is just one in a long line of African-American greats. Another name that is lauded in every nook and cranny of the globe, especially for his classic recording, "What a Wonderful World," is Louis Armstrong. Ellington and Armstrong did collaborate, but only during the final years of their lives.

Duke Ellington and Louis Armstrong on the far right.
https://commons.wikimedia.org/wiki/File:Billy_Strayhorn,_Duke_Ellington,_Leonard_Feather,_and_Louis_Armstrong,_1946.jpg

Their recording of "Duke Ellington Meets Louis Armstrong" in 1961 showed that both of them were still legends despite being past their prime. This eventually resulted in memorable renditions of classics like "Mood Indigo" and "Solitude." Their partnership bridged the worlds of swing and traditional jazz, creating timeless masterpieces that have become jazz lovers' all-time favorites today.

Ellington's other famous collaborations include:

- **Ella Fitzgerald:** Who doesn't know Ella Fitzgerald's "Dream a Little Dream of Me"? Duke Ellington's collaboration with the "First Lady of Song" produced some of the most memorable recordings in jazz. Their album, "Ella Fitzgerald Sings the Duke Ellington Song Book," featured Fitzgerald's beautiful vocals, which gave a sublime twist to Ellington's compositions. Together, they brought a new level of sophistication to jazz standards like "Take the 'A' Train" and "Caravan."

- **Billy Strayhorn:** Perhaps the most game-changing collaboration in Ellington's career was with composer and arranger Billy Strayhorn. Strayhorn's contributions to the Ellington repertoire included classics like "Take the 'A' Train" and "Lush Life." He helped define the well-known Ellington sound and solidified his status as a jazz innovator.

- **John Coltrane:** Duke Ellington's collaboration with saxophone legend John Coltrane gave rise to the album, "Duke Ellington & John Coltrane," which propelled their music eons ahead of time. Coltrane's distinctive style added a new dimension to Ellington's compositions, resulting in mesmerizing performances of tracks like "In a Sentimental Mood" and "Take the Coltrane." Their collaboration bridged the gap between traditional and modern jazz, influencing generations of musicians to come.

- **Count Basie:** The brainchild of two titans of swing, Duke Ellington and Count Basie, was the album "First Time! The Count Meets the Duke." Both of these greats were into big band jazz, but each had their unique style, with Basie's lean, bluesy arrangements complementing Ellington's lush orchestrations. Tracks like "Battle Royal" and "Jumpin' at the Woodside" are still hummed by swing lovers around the world.

His Magnificent Innovations

Time and again in this chapter and throughout history, Duke Ellington is hailed as an innovator of jazz. He excelled at the piano but was able to play virtually any jazz instrument. However, his singular compositions made him an innovator of the genre.

Ellington was a master of form, often composing extended works that went beyond the traditional three-minute jazz standard. He pioneered the use of suites in jazz, crafting multi-movement compositions that told complex narratives and explored a wide range of musical ideas. Examples include "Black, Brown, and Beige," "The Far East Suite," and

"Such Sweet Thunder."

His use of rich orchestral colors and textures, which he achieved through skillful orchestration and innovative use of instruments, was his defining point. His arrangements featured lush (opulent) harmonies, intricate counterpoint, and dynamic contrasts, creating a symphonic quality that set his music apart from traditional jazz.

In the world of music, Ellington is probably best known for transcending genres. He drew inspiration from a number of musical traditions where jazz formed only one part, like blues, classical, and folk. He seamlessly blended elements of these genres, creating a hybrid style that defied convention and expanded the possibilities of jazz. Many of his compositions were defined by complex harmonies, unconventional forms, and elevated orchestrations, blurring the line between jazz and classical music.

The best part is that he wasn't the only innovator in his band of musicians. Ellington's orchestra was renowned for its roster of virtuoso soloists, and he was a master at encouraging each musician's unique talents. His compositions included extended solo sections that allowed his band members to shine, highlighting their individual voices within the larger ensemble. This emphasis on individual expression and improvisation was a hallmark of Ellington's style and defined the role of the soloist in jazz.

Additionally, he was a master of rhythm, and his music was known for its infectious grooves and complex rhythmic patterns. He experimented with unconventional meters, syncopated rhythms, and polyrhythmic textures, creating a sense of forward momentum and swing that propelled his music forward.

A Glimpse into His Most Memorable Compositions

What made his compositions so great and innovative? The lyrics and melodies say it all!

"Sophisticated Lady"

"They say into your early life romance came
And in this heart of yours burned a flame
A flame that flickered one day and died away
Then, with disillusion deep in your eyes

You learned that fools in love soon grow wise

The years have changed you, somehow"

"Take the 'A' Train"

"You must take the 'A' train

To go to Sugar Hill way up in Harlem

If you miss the 'A' train

You'll find you missed the quickest way to Harlem"

"Mood Indigo"

"You ain't been blue, no, no, no

You ain't been blue

'Till you've had that mood indigo

That feelin' goes stealin' down to my shoes"

"It Don't Mean a Thing (If It Ain't Got That Swing)"

"It don't mean a thing, all you gotta do is sing

Do-wah, do-wah, do-wah, do-wah, do-wah, do-wah, do-wah, do-wah

It makes no difference if it's sweet or hot

Just keep that rhythm, give it everything you got"

His Quotes and His Praises

Duke Ellington wasn't only known for his musical compositions but also for his quotes and his thoughts against racial injustice.

"I don't believe in categories of any kind, and when you speak of problems between Blacks and whites in the U.S.A., you are referring to categories again. That indicates that you are considering a symptom and not the basic problem. The basic problem is greed, and at the bottom of all that greed is racial prejudice."

"What is music to you? What would you be without music? Music is everything. Nature is music (cicadas in the tropical night). The sea is music, the wind is music. The rain drumming on the roof and the storm raging in the sky are music. Music is the oldest entity. The scope of music is immense and infinite. It is the "esperanto" of the world."

Ellington was also known to joke around.

"I never had much interest in the piano until I realized that every time I played, a girl would appear on the piano bench to my left and another to my right."

Like every innovator throughout history, Ellington was slammed by critics of his time, but many also showered praises on him before and after his death.

"He was the pantheon of musical greats—the Beethovens, the Monteverdis, the Schoenbergs, the prime movers, the inspired innovators."

Gunther Schuler

"The master of them all is still Duke Ellington. The others, by comparison, are hardly more than composer-arrangers. Ellington is a composer, by which I mean, he comes nearer to knowing how to make a piece hang together than the others."

Aaron Copland

Chapter 5: Quiet Strength: Rosa Parks and the Montgomery Bus Boycott

"I have learned over the years that when one's mind is made up, this diminishes fear; knowing what must be done does away with fear."

Rosa Parks

During the 20th century, the American South existed in a state of twilight. It was a world cleaved in two, where the color of your skin dictated if you would walk to your new school or be driven to school by a school bus. Segregation in the South wasn't something new that popped up after the Civil War. It has a long history tied to race. Even before the war, the South ran on slavery, which basically meant White people were on the top and Black people were on the bottom. This wasn't a good era for people with Black skin.

Rosa Parks.

The Civil War may have ended slavery, but things were still a little messy afterward. The South had to figure out how to rejoin the country without slaves. During this confusing time, both the government and Southern states made new rules about giving Black people, who were now free, certain rights. The government had good intentions, but as expected, not everyone in the South liked the idea of Black people having equal rights. Some White people felt threatened by this change. To this set of people, those with Black skin were only meant to be slaves and not have a say in anything. So, Southern states started making new laws to keep Black people separate so they would remain obedient. They took away their right to vote to ensure they could never produce a Black leader. The segregation laws were born from the calculative minds of the White population in the Southern states who believed they were supreme; they were a way to keep things the way they were in the South before slavery ended.

The grandeur of the South stood in stark contrast to the daily indignities faced by African Americans. The Jim Crow Laws were the basis for the ban on interracial marriages at this time.

But it didn't end there.

Public spaces, from the halls of learning to the buses and taxis that the people traveled by fountains people drank from, and toilets to ease themselves, were segregated. This was a physical manifestation of the invisible lines that separated the two sets of people recognized in the world. "White" and "Colored" signs hung everywhere as a constant and cruel reminder of the systemic racism that was seen in every aspect of life within this era. This was the reality that Rosa Parks was faced with each day – a world where the very essence of her being, her dignity, was under constant attack simply for the color of her skin.

The Bloom of a Rose

Rosa Louise McCauley first entered the world on a beautiful day, the fourth of February 1913. Born in Tuskegee, Alabama, she was the daughter of separated parents – a hardworking carpenter, James McCauley, and a teacher, Leona Edwards. With her baby brother in tow, Rosa and her mother journeyed to Pine Level, a town near Montgomery, Alabama. There, they found refuge on her grandparents' farm.

Rosa's young self suffered at the hands of different illnesses, which led to her being a little stunted in growth. Though her early years were marked by struggle, Rosa found comfort in the strong arms of the African Methodist Episcopal Church. Until she turned eleven, her education took place within the loving walls of her own home, nurtured by her mother's teachings. Then came the Industrial School for Girls, a place where Rosa learned not just from books but also learned practical skills. Unfortunately, fate had other plans. Her grandmother fell ill, and Rosa had to make a tough choice, leaving school behind to care for the woman who had cared for her.

Everywhere young Rosa looked, she saw how the cruel laws separated Black and White folks in nearly every corner of life - restrooms, water fountains, schools, and even the buses they rode. White children got a fancy ride to school while Black children walked. Even on city buses, Blacks were forced to sit in the back – the "colored" section, far away from the Whites. It was a world of unfairness.

Rosa Parks' life takes shape against this backdrop with the echoes of slavery shadowing the generation before her. She lived a life defined by struggle but also by unwavering determination. As a young woman growing up in Alabama, she witnessed the injustices of segregation with clarity and conviction. Her spirit somehow remained unbroken, her resolve unyielding, even as her young mind figured out how to navigate a world that sought to confine her to the margins of society.

Rosa the Investigator

Rosa Parks met Raymond Parks in 1932 when she was 19. They got married and started a fulfilling life together. The two lovebirds ran the course of their union without producing children. Raymond was a barber and a member of the civil rights movement, the NAACP. Raymond was involved in trying to get better treatment for workers in Montgomery. He also helped collect money to defend nine Black teenagers who were wrongly accused of a crime.

With Raymond's help, Rosa got involved in fighting for the rights of Black citizens. In 1943, ignoring all of Raymond's advice to stay away from the civil rights movement, she joined the Montgomery chapter of the NAACP herself. She had a fire in her spirit. She was young and ready to fight for what was right.

In 1944, while Rosa worked with the National Association for the Advancement of Colored People, NAACP, a civil rights organization in Montgomery, she was asked to investigate the case of Recy Taylor. Aged 24 and a young Black mother, Taylor was abducted and gang raped by six White men. When Rosa came to ask her questions, the young mother told her how the men brutally used her, bruised her, and left her out in the cold blindfolded. What an act of inhumanity!

Rosa was so passionate about this case that she took it upon herself to launch a committee pushing for equal justice for Mrs. Recy Taylor. This was after she found out that the men mentioned were not arrested even after they confessed to the crime. She urged members of the committee to send letters of these types of crimes to the South in mass, and she even sent a personal letter with the committee's letterhead to the Governor on this issue. They only investigated the crime further but left the men roaming free. Rosa was heartbroken. It wasn't until several years later that the Alabama lawmakers finally owned up to the crime of failing to prosecute the offenders in the assault of Mrs. Taylor.

Rosa Stands Up, Sitting Down

Rosa Parks completed her high school education at the Highlander Folk School. The esteemed institution was a beacon of hope, teaching Black folks about their rights and equality. She learned just about enough to want to fight for her people's rights. The brutal murder of Emmett Till, a young Black boy who was just 14 years old, shook Rosa to the core. The teenage boy had been falsely accused of flirting with a White woman and, as a result, was murdered without a thought by White men. This senseless act, which was obviously fueled by racial hatred, cast a long shadow over Rosa. Like a sad movie, she kept playing it over and over again in her head, angry at the system for treating her people like they were worthless.

Four days after this incident, Rosa had just boarded a bus, tired and done with her day job of being a seamstress. All she wanted was to get home and be out of the way of the evidence of the segregation hanging over her head. She grabbed a seat beside a person of her skin color. Back in the 1950s, things were different in the Southern United States. There was a middle area where both could sit, but if a White person wanted a seat there, a Black person had to give it up.

While Rosa Parks and three other Black people were sitting in the middle area, a White person got on the bus, but the "White" section was already full, so he needed a seat. The driver, a man named James F. Blake, barked the order Rosa had heard countless times before, "Four seats up front for a White man!" He told all four Black people to move so the White person wouldn't have to sit next to them. The others got up, but Rosa Parks refused. She told them her feet were tired. However, that wasn't the case. She was tired indeed, not of walking but of being treated unfairly because of her skin color.

This was on the first day of December, and at this time, something inside Rosa had snapped. The years of humiliation and the quiet fading of her dignity all came together in a single, powerful NO. Her voice, usually soft, rang with steely resolve. She would not move. At that moment, she knew it was time to make a statement. A heavy silence hung thick in the air with anticipation buzzing. This wasn't just about a seat; it was about a lifetime of injustice – a fight for a future where Black people could ride the bus and live life itself with their heads held high. So, Rosa blatantly refused to stand up, which led to her arrest. She decided enough was enough. She remembered the unfortunate time the same bus driver had sent her off the bus because she had boarded through the wrong door. She was done playing it safe.

Birth of the Montgomery Bus Boycott

This was a world where a Black woman like Rosa could be addressed by her first name by a White child, where respect was a stranger, and courtesy was reserved solely for white skin. This simmering resentment, this quiet defiance, had been brewing in Rosa for years, a pressure building toward a single momentous act.

Montgomery had a Women's Political Council, which was made up of Black women. Rosa Parks was one of them. They were working to fight against the mistreatment of Black people on buses; some had even been arrested or killed for disobeying the driver's orders. Although Rosa wasn't the first to refuse to give up a seat, the Black population in the city saw her as the perfect example to rally behind because she was a respected citizen.

The Rosa Parks Bus.

English:Rmhermen at en.wikipediaItaliano: L'autore del caricamento è stato Rmhermen su en.wikipedia, CC BY-SA 3.0 <http://creativecommons.org/licenses/by-sa/3.0/>, via Wikimedia Commons. https://commons.wikimedia.org/wiki/File:Rosa_parks_bus.jpg

So, the Women's Political Council took action. They called for a boycott, asking all Black people in Montgomery to stop riding city buses on the day of Rosa's trial. And, on that Monday, a huge crowd – over forty thousand people – chose to walk or find other ways to get around. Meetings were held across the city later that evening, and the Black residents decided to keep boycotting the buses until things changed in the system. Their request was simple. They wanted Black bus drivers to be hired and for everyone to be able to sit anywhere on the bus without having to move for someone else.

The boycott lasted for a long time – 381 days, precisely. It was led by local leaders E.D. Nixon and a young minister named Martin Luther King Jr. Similar protests even started in other Southern cities. Finally, the highest court in the land, the Supreme Court, made a decision on Rosa's case in 1956. They ruled that separating people based on race on city buses was against the law. This decision came almost a year later, on November 13, 1956. The very next day after the court order arrived, on December 20, the Montgomery bus boycott ended.

Rosa Parks, along with Martin Luther King Jr., had started a movement based on peaceful protest in the South. This movement completely changed how people with different skin colors were treated in the United States. Martin Luther King Jr. became the voice of the movement, but sadly, he wouldn't live to see all the changes his work helped bring. However, Rosa Parks did, and she became a symbol of courage and standing up for what's right.

Montgomery's Defiant Rose – A Legacy of Courage

Rosa Parks' simple act of refusing to give up her bus seat to a White man became a spark that ignited a firestorm for justice. That spark was the Montgomery Bus Boycott, and it forever changed America. Her defiance wasn't some random outburst. It was a culmination of years of simmering frustration against the dehumanizing system of racial segregation. Black people were treated like second-class citizens, and Rosa said "no more" to that system of oppression, and in doing so, ignited a movement.

Rosa Parks, after getting arrested for refusing to give up her seat.
https://commons.wikimedia.org/wiki/File:Rosa_Parks_being_fingerprinted_by_Deputy_Sheriff_D.H._Lackey_after_being_arrested_on_February_22,_1956,_during_the_Montgomery_bus_boycott.jpg

The Montgomery Bus Boycott became a roar of defiance against a society that denied basic rights to Black people. For over a year, Black Montgomery residents walked, carpooled, or even braved the cold weather rather than ride segregated buses. This peaceful protest brought national attention to the ugliness of segregation.

The boycott came with formidable challenges. Black individuals were faced with pervasive hostility, intimidation, and, regrettably, instances of violence. However, they remained steadfast, and their unity showed how powerful collective action was. They stood resilient in the face of the relentless onslaught of adversity. They all had their minds made up. It was time to speak up for themselves, and they did so with their actions.

The Supreme Court's ruling in favor of the Black people was a victory not just for Montgomery but for the entire Civil Rights Movement. Today, Rosa Parks is the epitome of courage. Her story continues to inspire people to fight for what's right, speak truth to power, and never give up on the dream of equality. The Montgomery Bus Boycott stands as a testament to the fact that even ordinary people can achieve extraordinary things when they come together for a just cause.

Even after her famous bus incident, Rosa Parks kept fighting for civil rights. She worked for the NAACP and went to many civil rights events. Even though she became famous, she was a quiet person who didn't really like all the attention. But she used her fame for good. She wanted to help young people, especially Black children, have good lives. So, in 1987, she started a special school called the Rosa and Raymond Parks Institute for Self-Development. All her hard work fighting for equality didn't go unnoticed. Rosa Parks received two of the most important awards in the United States. President Clinton gave her the Presidential Medal of Freedom in 1996, and in 1999, she got the Congressional Gold Medal of Honor.

The Inspiration That Is Rosa Parks

Rosa Parks had no royal blood running through her veins. She wasn't a famous singer or a spirit-filled preacher. She was a quiet seamstress who, with a simple act, would forever alter the course of American history. Rosa's story stands as proof of the remarkable influence one person can have on their generation and history in general. The Montgomery Bus Boycott movement sparked a revolution, propelling the Civil Rights Movement forward and bringing hope to all who struggled for equality.

The story of Rosa Parks and the Montgomery Bus Boycott serves as a lasting source of inspiration for discussions on civil rights and activism, echoing through time in several profound ways:

- **Courage in the Face of Injustice:** Rosa Parks gave no room to fear. Well, maybe she was a little scared, but even knowing she might get in trouble, she wouldn't give up her seat on that bus. That simple act of defiance took guts. It showed everyone that even when things seem unfair, you can stand up for what's right. Her bold stance and bravery inspire us to do the same, encouraging individuals to confront injustice head-on, even when met with formidable obstacles.

- **Power of Peaceful Protest:** Following Parks' arrest, the Montgomery Bus Boycott came into play – a massive protest that started because of Rosa Parks. Black folks in Montgomery were tired of being treated differently on the buses, so they walked, choosing to brave the cold instead. It was a peaceful protest, but it was powerful. It showed everyone strength when people came together. The boycott became a compelling case study in effective activism strategies, showing how a peaceful protest can create real change.

- **Role of Individuals in Civil Rights Movements:** Rosa Parks was no big-shot politician or anything. She was a regular person, just like you and me. Her story proves that anyone can make a difference no matter who they are. We all have the power to fight for what's fair. We all have a pivotal role to play as individuals, irrespective of societal status.

- **The Struggle for Equality:** Rosa Parks' battles against racial segregation and discrimination did not end. The fight for equality isn't over yet. Racism and unfair treatment are still part of our modern-day world. But, from Rosa Parks' story, we now know how far we've come and how much further we need to go. It's a call to action for a new generation to keep pushing for a world where everyone is treated equally, no matter the color of their skin.

Rosa Parks' story is a powerful message for equality and justice – a guiding light for anyone fighting for civil rights. It provides us with a historical backdrop, proves that peaceful protests can work, and reminds us that even regular people can make a big difference. Her bravery teaches us valuable lessons that will continue to reverberate within the collective consciousness of humanity, inspiring generations to keep fighting for a world where everyone is treated fairly and with respect.

Famous Quotes

"Whatever my individual desires were to be free, I was not alone. There were many others who felt the same way."

-Rosa Parks

"People always say that I didn't give up my seat because I was tired, but that isn't true. I was not tired physically, or no more tired than I usually was at the end of a working day. I was not old, although some people have an image of me as being old then. I was forty-two. No, the only tired I was, was tired of giving in."

-Rosa Parks

Chapter 6: Literary Luminary: Maya Angelou's Words of Wisdom

What would the literary world look like without the works of the great Maya Angelou? Maya was more than just a poet; she was a civil rights activist, a hero, and the voice of a generation who spoke for African American people. She used her talent to inspire other women and make a difference in the world.

She cemented her name among some of the greatest poets in the world with poems like *Still I Rise, Caged Bird, On the Pulse of Morning,* and more.

This chapter covers the life of a great woman whose words still echo to this day.

Maya Angelou.

Maya Angelou's Early Life

Marguerite Ann Johnson, AKA Maya Angelou, was born in St. Louis, Missouri, on April 4, 1928. She got the name "Maya" from her older brother, Bailey Johnson Jr. When she was born, Bailey had a stutter and couldn't pronounce her name correctly, so he called her "My" as in "My sister."

One time, he was reading a book about the Mayan civilization. He liked the name so much and thought "Maya" would be the perfect nickname for his sister. Little did he know that this would be a name the whole world would know.

Maya had a very hard life and a traumatizing childhood. Her parents had a troubling marriage and divorced when she was only three years old. Her life changed drastically after that event. She and her brother, Bailey, with whom she shared a close bond, went to live with their parental grandmother, Anne Henderson, in Stamps, Arkansas.

Maya's new life was challenging. Stamps was a white community, and she and her brother suffered from injustice and racism. When Maya was only four or five years old, she was introduced to the real world and saw what life was like for Black people. Every day, she would hear a comment or face a situation that destroyed her confidence and broke her heart.

When Maya was eight, she visited her mother and stayed with her for a while. What happened during that visit changed Maya's life forever. Her mother was dating a horrible man named Freeman. Freeman sexually assaulted and raped Maya in her own house, the first place she called home and the only place she should have felt safe.

Maya spoke about the traumatizing incident in her 1969 autobiography, "I Know Why the Caged Bird Sings." She said, "The act of rape on an eight-year-old body is a matter of the needle giving because the camel can't. The child gives because the body can, and the mind of the violator cannot."

Freeman was arrested and found guilty, but he only stayed in prison for one day. When he got out, Maya's uncles killed him to avenge their young niece. Maya blamed herself for his death and believed that it was her words, saying that he raped her, that killed him.

The rape and the murder were too much for any child to handle. Maya was traumatized and couldn't speak for five years. As a young child with little understanding of the world, Maya believed that her voice was powerful enough to kill a man. She was terrified that if she spoke again, more people would die.

Maya would find out later in life how powerful her voice truly was and its impact on the world.

Maya returned to Stamps, where she lived with her brother and grandmother. During these five years, she retreated within herself. She didn't allow anyone near her except her brother.

Racism's Ugly Face

The racism Maya witnessed in Stamps shaped her voice and storytelling. She saw the inhumane treatment and the heartless crimes committed against Black people every day. The white community denied them their identity. Maya refused to be a victim of her circumstances and stood up against injustice from a very young age.

She worked as a maid for a wealthy white woman. The woman refused to call her Maya and called her Mary instead. Maya felt that she needed to protect her identity, and she corrected the woman multiple times, saying that her name was Maya.

However, the woman ignored her and continued with her intolerant behavior. Maya couldn't handle it anymore. In a powerful and rebellious move, Maya broke the woman's plates and quit.

Maya was seeing racism's ugly face everywhere she looked. She had a terrible toothache once, and her grandmother, Annie, took her to the dentist. He was white and refused to treat a Black girl. Annie and Maya had to travel a long distance to find a Black dentist to help her.

Maya's experience with racism and the brutality she and her brother were exposed to scarred them. Many Black women felt that their place in the world was carved out, and they would continue living under oppression. However, Maya was different. Before she held her pen to write, in her mind, she wrote her own story. It wasn't one of a defeated girl who gave in to her circumstances but of a strong girl who was ready to defy an ignorant society.

Maya's love for literature and writing began at a young age when she was living in Arkansas. She was a big fan of Edgar Allan Poe and William Shakespeare, and she memorized their poems. She also wrote her own poetry when she was still a child, showcasing her immense talent and prophesying the great future that was awaiting her.

Maya refused to let an intolerant and bigot society define her. She was resilient and adamant to change the narrative and follow her dreams. Living in a white community that tried to silence Black people, Maya found her voice in writing.

A New Beginning

When Maya turned 13, she and Bailey moved to San Francisco to live with their mother. During this time, Maya had regained her voice and started talking. San Francisco provided an opportunity for Maya to start over and let go of the shackles of her traumatic past. She attended Mission High School, where she won a scholarship to study drama and dance at Labor School in San Francisco.

During her time at Labor School, she was introduced to progressive ideals that impacted her political activism. In 1942, Maya dropped out of school to become the first African American female cable car conductor in the state.

Her desire for education was powerful, and she returned to school and graduated in 1944.

Guy Johnson

In her senior year of high school, Maya had a short relationship with a young man and became pregnant. At the age of 17 and shortly after graduation, she gave birth to her only son, Clyde Bailey (Guy) Johnson, whom she named after her brother.

This wasn't the life Maya had envisioned for herself. However, she didn't abandon her son or neglect his needs. She moved out of her mother's home to start her life as a single mother.

She didn't ask her family for money or support. She worked as a cook and a waitress to provide for her son. However, Maya didn't let her responsibilities distract her from her love for poetry, dance, and music.

Maya's Many Talents

In 1952, Maya married a Greek sailor, Anastasios Angelopoulos. Then, she started her nightclub singing career and called herself Maya Angelou, taking her husband's last name. However, their marriage didn't last, and they got divorced after three years.

Maya's life finally changed for the better. Her singing career flourished, and she joined the opera, performing Porgy and Bess in America and Europe.

She was also a dancer and studied under Martha Graham, a dancing icon that Time magazine called "Dancer of the Century." She performed multiple dances on TV with American dancer Alvin Ailey.

Maya was also a successful singer. She wrote many songs and recorded her first album, Calypso Lady, in 1957.

In 1959, Maya moved to New York to join the Harlem Writers Guild, a group of African American writers who supported Black authors associated with the Civil Rights Movement.

Finding Love and Exploring the World

In New York, Maya met South African lawyer and civil rights activist Vusumzi Make. The couple fell in love right away, and she traveled with Make to Cairo, Egypt, where she worked as an editor at The Arab Observer.

Maya and Vusumzi broke up a year later, and she moved with her son to Ghana. She was a writer at The Ghanaian Times, an editor at The African Review, and an assistant administrator at the University of Ghana's School of Music and Drama. She also worked with the African American expatriate's group.

It seemed like Maya's schedule was full. However, the brilliant poet still found time to learn Arabic, French, Italian, and Spanish.

Friendship with Malcolm X

Maya and Malcolm first met in 1961 when she was still living in New York. She described him using poetic language that only the great Maya Angelou could think of: "His aura was too bright, and his masculine force affected me physically. A hot desert storm eddied around him and rushed to me, making my skin contract and my pores slam shut...his hair was the color of burning embers, and his eyes pierced."

In 1964, they met in Ghana. They were often accompanied by other great minds like American writer W.E.B. Du Bois.

Malcolm was getting ready to build the Organization of Afro-American Unity to address racial problems in America. He was impressed by Maya's brilliant mind and dedication to fighting racism. He wanted her to join his organization. He convinced her to leave Ghana and return to the U.S. so they could work together to help oppressed Black Americans.

When Malcolm returned to the U.S., he and Maya kept in touch and corresponded with each other. Maya often gave him helpful advice. In one of her letters, she told him to speak to the people like he was one of them and avoid talking over their heads. Malcolm appreciated her feedback and was very impressed with her insights. He wrote back, saying that she had a great soul and was down to earth and that these qualities made her special.

Malcolm's sweet words touched Maya greatly, and she was eager to leave Ghana and join his organization.

After one month, Maya returned home. Their friendship was so strong that he wanted to pick her up from the airport, but she told him she was visiting family in San Francisco. However, these two great friends never saw each other again. On February 21, 1965, Malcolm was assassinated.

Friendship with Dr. Martin Luther King

Maya continued her work as a civil rights activist. Shortly after Malcolm's death, she met Dr. Martin Luther King. King reached out to her to act as the Southern Christian Leadership Conference coordinator, a civil rights organization. Maya was excited to work with King.

However, her joy didn't last. Dr. King was assassinated, and in a cruel twist of fate, the incident took place on Maya's birthday. Maya was devastated when she heard the news. Her birthday was no longer a happy occasion, and she stopped celebrating it for years as it was associated with the death of a good friend and an American hero. For 30 years, she would send a flower bouquet to King's wife on the anniversary of his death.

After King's passing, Maya focused more on her writing and continued working with civil rights organizations, which inspired many of her poems.

One of her most popular poems is *"On the Pulse of Morning,"* which discusses themes such as historical pain, reconciliation, and responsibility. It encourages Black and white people to reconcile with the past and end ignorance and violence.

> *"Come, clad in peace and I will sing the songs*
> *The Creator gave to me when I*
> *And the tree and stone were one.*
> *Before cynicism was a bloody sear across your brow*
> *And when you yet knew you still knew nothing.*
> *The river sings and sings on."*

In 1993, Maya read this poem at Bill Clinton's inauguration.

I Know Why the Caged Bird Sings

Novelist James Baldwin comforted Maya after the passing of Martin Luther King Jr. He was the one who encouraged her to seek comfort in her literary work. She started writing her autobiography, *"I Know Why the Caged Bird Sings."* It was honest and raw, telling of her life starting from her childhood until the birth of her son. She talked about all the challenges she faced as a young Black woman in a white community. She also discussed her traumatic experience with her mother's boyfriend and its impact on her life.

Maya Angelou's autobiography.

The title of her book is a line from *"Sympathy,"* a poem by American poet Paul Laurence Dunbar.

"I know why the caged bird sings, ah me,
When his wing is bruised and his bosom sore —
When he beats his bars, and he would be free."

Maya found inspiration in Dunbar's words because they are the perfect analogy to Black people's desire for freedom from oppression. The story is about a caged bird who sings and flaps its wings because it is sad and wants to be free from the cage that is killing its spirit.

Maya was also like a bird when she lived in Arkansas. Stamps was her cage, where people tried to erase her identity. While the bird sang and flapped its wings, Maya broke dishes and stood tall, refusing to allow anyone to imprison her spirit.

In the poem, the bird wounded itself while failing to escape from the cage. However, Maya didn't spend her whole life like a caged bird; instead, she found her freedom by escaping from Arkansas.

In 1970, Maya published her autobiography, which was an instant success. It was a New York Times bestseller for two years and was nominated for a National Book Award.

Huge Success

Maya became a national figure, and many found her words inspiring and courageous. Her poetry is an anthem of freedom and resilience. Poems like *"Still I Rise"* showcase Maya's brilliant word choice, which reflects powerful emotions.

"Out of the huts of history's shame
I rise
Up from a past that's rooted in pain
I rise
I'm a Black ocean, leaping and wide,
Welling and swelling I bear in the tide.
Leaving behind nights of terror and fear
I rise
Into a daybreak that's wondrously clear
I rise"

The poem reflects how Maya rose from racism, oppression, and her dark and traumatic past to become one of the world's most famous poets. It also symbolizes African Americans' struggles during the Civil Rights era and their search for freedom and equality. Repeating the phrase, *"Still I Rise,"* reflects Maya's resilience and strength.

Maya was a lecturer and teacher who inspired students all over the country. In 1972, she wrote the screenplay and composed the score for the movie Georgia, Georgia. It was the first-ever screenplay by a female African American to be produced.

Maya wrote 36 books and about 167 poems. She was nominated for a Pulitzer and was awarded the Presidential Medal of Freedom. She reached international fame and everyone around the world now knows her name.

Creative Process

Creating masterpieces like Maya's poems is a process. She didn't just sit on her couch and write. She had some strange rules for writing.

Hotel Rooms

Although Maya had a big home, she preferred writing in empty and quiet hotel rooms with no TV or wall art to avoid distractions. In an interview with Oprah, Maya said that she needed to find a quiet place inside her to hear her thoughts.

She would arrive there at dawn, usually at 5:30 a.m., to write. She would lie on the bed with a pen and paper and let the words flow.

Sherry

At 6:15 a.m., Maya would drink a small glass of sherry. Once she got in the zone, she wouldn't have another drink as she entered her world and wanted to stay focused.

Bible

Maya was a wordsmith, but she still needed inspiration. She often kept a Judaic Bible and a Christian Bible as she enjoyed the word choice and music in the verses. She also used a thesaurus and a dictionary.

Early Bird

Maya was an early bird. She woke up at 5 a.m. every day and arrived at her hotel room at 6:30 a.m. to start working.

Maya's Legacy in Contemporary Literature

Maya wasn't just the voice of her generation; she is the voice of every generation. Her views and poems are still relevant to this day. She left a huge mark in the literary world with her poems and books, which are taught in schools and universities worldwide.

She is a role model for African Americans who, for centuries, have lived in a society that is continuously trying to silence them and make them believe their voices don't matter.

Her powerful themes still speak to many young African Americans who can relate to her struggles. They feel that every poem she wrote perfectly describes their lives in a society that still has much to learn about equality.

Angelou's Still I Rise.

Maya's experience as a young Black woman resonates with many African Americans today who are still struggling with intolerance and oppression. Reading poems like *"Still I Rise"* empowers them and makes them believe that no matter what they face, they won't be broken down or defeated. They will always rise.

Maya's literary works have been translated into many languages, influencing people from different cultures and backgrounds.

As a victim of sexual abuse, Maya was brave to tell her story, encouraging women of different races to speak up and demand justice.

Maya also impacted modern culture. She wrote movie scripts, guest-starred on popular TV shows like Sesame Street, and appeared on talk shows like The Tonight Show. She also had a prominent role on the legendary TV show *Roots.*

Maya departed this world on May 28th, 2014, leaving a legacy that will survive the test of time. For centuries to come, people will talk about her, and her name will be mentioned in the literary world with poets like William Wordsworth and Emily Dickinson.

Chapter 7: The Gentle Warrior: Desmond Tutu's Peaceful Crusade

Archbishop Desmond Tutu was not a political leader; he was a servant of God who didn't lust after power. This quality allowed him to call out injustices on all sides. His fight for equality and liberation never came with army boots and a gun. Instead, he picked up a Bible, a pen, and a mic and managed to shift the world.

The only time Desmond Tutu lifted his hands was to stop a fight. His palms would never be up to hurt someone or to surrender. As a peaceful warrior, his words were his sword to defend and his bandage to heal. The Archbishop stood as a righteous representation of how the same religion that oppressed Africans could free them.

Desmond Tutu.

For Desmond Tutu, the mission for peace was never finished. When South Africa finally overcame the injustices of apartheid, he ensured a peaceful transition with the Truth and Reconciliation Commission. The Archbishop broadened his mind and looked to the global stage to condemn atrocities around the world and to actively progress to make change. For this powerful clergyman, remaining silent was not an option. At great risk to himself, he always spoke the truth and stood for what was right.

Apartheid South Africa: Discrimination as the Law

A stranger grips his trench coat as the wind scrapes his ashy knuckles. He looks frantically left and right for a taxi to get him home. It's been a long day at work. He squints as the orange sun reflects off a nearby window. He turns, running to the corner as the taxi picks up some passengers. His run is halted by a giant hand gripping the back of his collar.

The officer's beige uniform sends shivers down through the stranger's body. The officer demands a work pass. He fumbles, shivering from fear, clumsily hitting every pocket of his winter layers. Finally, he pulls out the book. The officer examines the pass with laser focus. He shoves the book into the stranger's chest, pushing him along his way by finishing off the exchange with a racial slur, just for good measure.

The discriminatory laws of the apartheid system were the culmination of the oppressive racial attitudes of colonization. Resources were unevenly shared along racial lines, and varying laws were applied to different races. The best areas were reserved for white people, while other groups were shoved into racial slums. People were forcibly displaced from their ancestral lands and thrown into new lives they never asked for.

In this volatile environment, mission schools emerged to spread the Gospel to Africans and to educate them in the civilized ways of Europeans. Painting Africans as lesser people who needed saving by the church was an additional tool for the oppression of Black people. The Christian doctrine was a justification for discrimination. However, in the Bible, there are teachings of love, compassion, liberation, and treating neighbors with kindness. So, like Christianity, it could be used to oppress, but it could also be applied to peace, justice, and liberation.

Religious leaders play an important role in the moral guidance of a nation. Clergy people dedicated to the service of God are required to represent those who suffer the most. Through his letters, speeches, and activism, Desmond Tutu embodied the moral heartbeat of Christianity. He courageously used his powerful voice and spiritual ethics to call out injustice wherever he saw it. His work in charity, commitment to education, and strong moral character drove this hero to greatness.

Early Life

Desmond Tutu was born in Klerksdorp on October 7, 1931. His father, Zachariah, was educated in a mission school and was a Headmaster in the Western Transvaal, which is today the North West Province of South Africa. His mother, Aletha Mohlare, worked as a cleaner. He was one of four children.

When Tutu was eight, his dad was transferred to teach at a multiracial school for African, Indian, and Colored students in Ventersdorp. This was when Tutu started attending the African Methodical Episcopal Church with his sister. His father was transferred again, this time to Roodpeoort, where the family lived in a shack.

In 1943, the family was forced out of their home due to the apartheid laws. They found themselves in Munsieville, a township designated for Black people in Krugersdorp. Tutu developed an entrepreneurial spirit. His bare feet would send dust clouds into the air as they pounded the streets to the wholesale store where he could buy oranges to sell at a profit. He would also go from door to door, tirelessly knocking to promote his mother's laundry service, where they would pick up, wash, and deliver clothing. Tutu sold peanuts and would later become a caddy for tips at Killarney Golf Course.

In 1945, he enrolled in Western High Government Secondary School. During his final year, he was devastated by a terrible case of tuberculosis. The disease kept his back glued to a hospital bed for an entire year. There, he met Father Trevor Huddleston, who further encouraged Tutu's spiritual inclinations. Huddleston regularly brought Tutu books and eventually accepted him as a server in the Munsieville parish.

Tutu's close relationship with Father Huddleston led him to meet Pastor Makhene and Father Sekgaphane, who were instrumental in admitting him to the Anglican church where he would spend his career as a clergyman. In 1950, Tutu matriculated despite being massively behind with the coursework due to his illness. He was then accepted into Witwatersrand Medical School but was unable to attend due to finances.

Tutu opted to follow his father into teaching. He obtained his qualification at Bantu Normal College and went on to get a Bachelor of Arts at the University of South Africa. The struggle hero, Robert Sobukwe, who was the leader of the Pan Africanist Congress (or the

PAC), assisted Tutu with his studies.

Discrimination and Spiritual Evolution

How can one reconcile religion with oppression? Clergymen from the pulpit supported the apartheid laws. Many churches held different racially separated masses. White supremacists believed that Black people could not be redeemed because they were demonic or more animal than human.

Black people were considered so racially contaminated that they could not have a church with white people to worship the same God who created everyone. Staring into the face of so-called God-fearing people while holding these racist attitudes can either discourage someone or give them the motivation to transform society.

Desmond Tutu's heart was focused on the service of the Lord from a young age. His mission-educated father and devout mother instilled Christian values for as long as he could remember. His deeply held beliefs and his father's drive for education propelled Tutu to study the intricacies of his faith. When he first started teaching at Munsieville High School in 1955, he was already thinking about becoming a priest. In the same year, he got married to Nomalizo Leah Shenxane, who was one of his father's favorite students.

This is also where the injustices of apartheid became clearer for the future Archbishop. In 1953, the Bantu Education Act was signed into legislation. It outlined that education provided to Black people would be of lower quality than that given to their white counterparts. This was to prepare the population for racialized roles that the discriminatory government carved out. After staying for three years to finish teaching the students he had already taken on, Tutu left the profession in protest.

The pull toward religious service became stronger. In 1958, he became a subdeacon in Krugersdorp. He then enrolled in St. Peter's Theological College in Rossentenville, which was run by the Fathers of the Community of the Resurrection. Tutu's passion for his faith allowed him to flourish. He was a top student, obtaining his Licentiate in Theology with two distinctions.

He would work his way up from deacon with his compassion, love, charity, and prowess for organizing to Archbishop. Throughout his journey, Tutu was constantly challenged to align his activism with his faith. As a morally upstanding man, his judgment was always fair, equally condemning or praising all sides of a disagreement. Tutu never let loyalty or friendships shake his values. He would speak out against his own if he believed they were wrong.

Challenges with the Church and Government

Once Desmond Tutu started lecturing at the University of Botswana, Lesotho, and at Swaziland, which was located in Lesotho, he was introduced to Black Theology. This idea asserts that the dominant culture has corrupted Christianity to serve their agendas. Black Theology asks the fundamental question at the center of Christianity: who does God biblically side with – the *oppressors* or the *oppressed?* Through the teachings of Black Theology, Tutu found a way to marry his faith and his activism by using morality to criticize oppressive systems.

With this new social justice lens, Tutu returned to England in 1971. Dr. Walter Carson, the Acting Director of the Theological Education Fund, invited Tutu to be part of a shortlist for the Associate Director for Africa position. This allowed him to travel to many disadvantaged nations around the world. Tutu was especially excited to travel to African nations.

After six months of travel, he returned to South Africa in 1975 to take up the post of the first Black Anglican Dean of Johannesburg and become the Rector of St. Mary's Cathedral. At this point, the struggle against the apartheid regime was intensifying, with violence and tyranny skyrocketing in the country.

During the height of South African instability in the 1980s, Desmond Tutu became the Archbishop of Cape Town.

On June 16, 1976, the Soweto uprising broke out. The ground of the township shook as students took to the streets in protest of being forced to learn in Afrikaans, which they saw as the language of the oppressor. The police fired live rounds into the crowd of children, killing many of the youth in attendance. Education was an issue close to Desmond Tutu's heart, and he cared dearly for the children of South Africa. The news of the uprising grieved and stunned the religious leader.

In his sorrow, he put together the Soweto Parents Crisis Committee, which was started in order to protect and uplift young people. In 1976, Desmond Tutu wrote an open letter to Prime Minister John Vorster. In it, Tutu reminds Vorster of the struggle that the Afrikaans people faced to grow their power nation in South Africa. He then compares their struggle to the hardships Black people were facing in the country. He used this comparison to call for a peaceful solution for the liberation of Black people, warning that violent protests could spring up at any time. The apartheid government replied by dismissing the letter as propaganda.

During the height of South African instability in the 1980s, Desmond Tutu became the Archbishop of Cape Town. He was the first Black leader of a province in South Africa in the Anglican church. 10,000 people gathered for the Eucharist in his honor. Although he had become accustomed to it, criticism of his views still circulated in mainstream media. Multiple Heads of State congratulated him, and the president of the ANC, Oliver Tambo, sent his congratulations from exile.

The Pulpit for Change

Desmond Tutu's priestly career of activism during apartheid focused on four main tenets. First, he wanted equal rights for all the citizens of the country. Second, he wanted the pass laws abolished. Third, he sought the same level of education for all South Africans, regardless of race. Last, he wanted the system of forced relocation to end.

The white mainstream constantly flung criticism at Desmond Tutu. According to them, as a man of God, he was not supposed to be stirring the political pot. However, he used the pulpit for his activism because it aligned with how he understood the teachings of Christ. In 1983, the military machine of the apartheid government awoke the neighborhood of Mogopa with bright lights through bedroom windows. The neighborhood was displaced to the homeland of Bophuthatswan.

Upon hearing about the destruction, Tutu brought together church leaders and priests, including Dr. Allan Boesak. They performed an all-night vigil on the land and condemned the actions of the government. Tutu appealed to the Christian values of the conservative Afrikaner population to call out the atrocities of apartheid.

He balanced his criticism of the government with praise. For example, when the Minster of Police, Louis le Grange, allowed political prisoners to continue their education behind bars, Tutu congratulated him. Trying to keep the peace, Tutu explained that locking up political protesters increased the chances of rioting and violent uprisings. His understanding of Christian love never allowed bitterness to grow in the clergyman's heart. He was committed to calling out sin wherever he saw it and blowing the winds of progress with honest words.

Desmond Tutu idealistically imagined a bright future for South Africa's Black population. A hailstorm of criticism hit Tutu yet again when he stated that there would be a Black prime minister within 10 years. The conservative white population condemned his comments as outrageous and illogical.

To make progress toward racial inclusion, the apartheid government proposed an electoral college that would include Indians and *Colored people* but would still exclude Black Africans who were at the bottom of the racial ladder. Desmond Tutu stood vocally against this, garnering support from all racial groups to condemn the electoral college.

His work in education never ceased. He was still a member of the Soweto Parents Crisis Committee, which he helped found. In 1985, at a conference at the University of Witwatersrand, Tutu warned that the lack of education among the youth was concerning. He said that the uneducated youth would lead to a liberation movement that was not ready to occupy positions of power after apartheid ended.

Mobilizing church leadership quickly became Desmond Tutu's specialty. Tutu marched with other clergymen to release the minister, John Thorne, who spoke out against apartheid. Tutu and the other priests were arrested under the Riotous Assemblies Act. This campaign put his life in danger.

Tutu was attacked from all angles with bomb scares, death threats, and reputation damage. His persistence led to a meeting with Prime Minister PW Botha and his delegation. This was the first time a Black person outside of the political system met with white South African leaders. However, no progress was made in these talks. For his constant fight for peace against the oppressive regime, Tutu received the Nobel Peace Prize in 1984. His constant traveling made him a global icon who brought the world's attention to political prisoners like Nelson Mandela.

Tutu was not afraid to unite with those who had common political goals. In 1983, he joined a coalition of Black Consciousness groups, including the PAC, to launch the National Forum. Then, in August 1983, he became the Patron of the United Democratic Front (or the UDF). This group was a political party opposed to the discriminatory system of the time.

As a respected family man, his wife, Leah, walked by his side every step of the way. Her political contributions complemented those of her husband. Leah campaigned for better working conditions for domestic workers. She also helped start the South African Domestic Workers Association.

Tutu never reserved his compassion or condemnation for only one group. He equally applied his moral standards to all situations. In Duduza, in 1985, Desmond Tutu collaborated with Bishops Simeon Nkoane and Kenneth Oram to stop a Black police officer from being murdered. A crowd accused the officer of being a spy for the government and were adamant about killing him. They managed to save his life. Tutu then used the pulpit of a funeral to condemn violence from all sides, whether it was the police or the population.

His compassion for the people made his focus broad. Tutu eventually shifted his focus to health concerns like tuberculosis and HIV in South Africa. He set up the Desmond Tutu HIV Foundation, which helped fund New Somerset Hospital. The public clinic was one of the first places to provide anti-retroviral therapy.

Global Peace and Social Justice

Desmond Tutu's fair judgment and forgiving nature led him to chair the Truth and Reconciliation Commission (TRC). This body was set up after the first democratic election in 1994 to allow the perpetrators of human rights violations to confess their crimes and be pardoned. Victims were also allowed to tell their stories. This was done to help heal the wounds of apartheid and facilitate forgiveness according to Tutu's Christian beliefs. He retired as the Archbishop of Cape Town and put all his efforts into the TRC. Later, he was given the title Archbishop

Emeritus.

His efforts for peace didn't stop at South Africa's borders. Having had the opportunity to travel the world, Desmond Tutu was globally minded. During the apartheid era, he built continental bridges by thanking leaders in Zimbabwe, Lesotho, Botswana, and Mozambique for welcoming refugees. He also asked them to refrain from chasing away the South Africans in need.

His commitment to peace led to the creation of the Desmond Tutu Peace Centre, or the DTPC, which he co-founded with his wife, Leah Tutu. The organization was dedicated to leveraging the influence the Archbishop had for world peace. Tutu was focused on speaking against injustice in all forms, stating, *"If you are neutral in situations of injustice, you have chosen the side of the oppressor."*

One of his most popular international stances was his position on the Israel and Palestine conflict. He pleaded with the Israeli government to stop bombing Beirut and appealed to Palestinian leader Yasser Arafat to be more reasonable in his expectations of Israel and its right to exist as a nation-state.

Tutu condemned the treatment of prisoners in Guantanamo Bay during the War on Terror. He stood with the Burmese people to call out human rights abuses in the country. He also demanded the release of the Burmese opposition leader, Aung San Suu Kyi. Remaining fair and honest, he then criticized Suu Kyi for her silence on the genocide of Rohingya Muslims in Myanmar. Tutu would also condemn the ANC government he once defended for its flaws and would compare Robert Mugabe's Zimbabwean government to the apartheid regime.

Tutu's Legacy

Desmond Tutu passed away in 2021 at the age of 80. He worked for global peace until his last breath. His legacy carries on in those who peacefully stand firm and advocate bravely without violence. Upholding strong values and applying them evenly underpinned the Archbishop's activism. He saw all people as one and wanted the best for everyone through the love his Christian faith promoted. Desmond Tutu lives on as a symbol of forgiveness, peace, and unity.

Plaque honoring Desmond Tutu.

Chapter 8: Fields of Freedom: George Washington Carver's Agricultural Genius

George Washington Carver was a child born into slavery. Following the Civil War, he became a prominent figure in the scientific community. He made history as the first Black man to earn a graduate degree in agriculture.

Carver's expertise in botany became widely recognized. He gained fame for his groundbreaking work with peanuts and various other plants, which led to the development of innovative products derived from them.

George Washington Carver.

In addition to his scientific interests, Carver was a passionate educator. He shared his knowledge with students and farmers alike. Despite his significant achievements, he remained remarkably humble. He was offered a lot of money for his discoveries but chose not to take it.

Early Life

George Carver's story begins in Missouri, where he was born into slavery around 1864, during the Civil War. His exact birth date remains unknown. His mother, Mary, was also a slave on the farm owned by Moses and Susan Carver. Meanwhile, George's father, also a slave on a different farm, tragically died in a wagon accident shortly before George's birth. George had two older sisters and a brother, Jim, but sadly, he never got to know his sisters.

One night, when George was just a baby suffering from a bad cough, their lives took a dramatic turn. Slave raiders burst into their home, forcibly taking Mary, George, and one of his sisters away, with intentions to sell them to other slave owners. Despite exhaustive searches, the Carvers could only find and bring George back home; Mary and his sister remained lost.

Left orphaned at a young age, George and Jim found family with Moses and Susan Carver, whom they lovingly referred to as Aunt and Uncle. Moses and Susan, immigrants from Germany who had settled in Missouri to start a farm, provided a nurturing environment for the boys, always encouraged George's thirst for knowledge, and treated the boys like their own.

Because of his health issues, George couldn't help with field work like Jim. Instead, he helped around the house, and especially in the garden, where he felt most at home. George's deep love for nature blossomed during his childhood. He spent countless hours outdoors and threw himself into the study of plants, which is when he developed an intuitive understanding of their needs and intricacies. He planted his own garden in the woods, where he nursed sick plants back to health. Word of George's remarkable talent spread, earning him the nickname "Plant Doctor." Proud of this recognition, George continued to pursue his passion for botany despite facing racial discrimination when he sought educational opportunities. Even after the abolition of slavery, George encountered numerous obstacles due to the color of his skin and struggled to gain admission to college.

School and College Studies

George was eager to learn, even at a young age. At eleven, he asked to go to school, hungry for more knowledge beyond what Aunt Susan had taught him at home. Unfortunately, the nearby school in Diamond was only for white children, leaving George with no choice but to move eight miles away to Neosho, where a school for Black children existed.

He packed his bags and bid farewell to Moses, Susan, and Jim. Despite the uncertainty of where he would live, George's focus was solely on his education. Luck was on his side when he met Mariah and Andrew Watkins in Neosho. They kindly offered George a place to stay while he attended school, only asking for help with chores in return for room and board.

George immersed himself in his studies and worked hard both in school and at home, often reading late into the night after finishing his chores. After four years, he had mastered all that his school had to offer, and George knew it was time to move on to a more challenging environment.

He said goodbye to the Watkinses and relocated to Kansas for further schooling. There, he juggled various odd jobs while pursuing his studies and self-educating by reading different literature. It was during his high school years in Kansas that he adopted the middle name 'Washington' to honor the first president of the United States.

After high school, he was accepted to Highland College in Kansas but was denied admission upon arrival due to his race. However, this only temporarily crushed his dreams. George was undeterred even after this and continued his studies independently while managing his own farm, but he soon realized his true calling lay elsewhere. So, he reapplied to college and was accepted to Simpson College in Iowa, where his race mattered little compared to his academic abilities.

After graduating from Iowa Agricultural College in 1894, George became the first African American to teach at what would later become Iowa State University. However, his life took a significant turn when Booker T. Washington offered him a teaching position at the Tuskegee Institute in April 1896, igniting George's passion for helping farmers and revolutionizing agricultural practices for African Americans.

Tuskegee Institute

One day, Booker T. Washington, a well-known African American leader, paid a visit to George Carver. He had an important proposal: to join the Tuskegee Institute, a school dedicated to educating African Americans. Although the position wouldn't bring in much money, it offered George the chance to share his knowledge about farming and plants with others.

George Carver's journey from the lush fields of Iowa to the cotton plantations of the South was marked by a stark realization of the region's reality. As he looked out of the train window, he saw scraggly cotton fields, lonely vegetables, and exhausted land.

Before the Civil War, cotton was king in the South, fueled by slave labor and the invention of the cotton gin. This led to an endless cycle of cotton production, with plantations relying on vast quantities of slaves to meet the demand. Despite the war's end and the abolition of slavery, the "cotton culture" persisted.

The Tuskegee Faculty Council with George Washington and Booker T. Washington.
https://commons.wikimedia.org/wiki/File:The_Tuskegee_Faculty_Council,_1902.jpg

Arriving in Tuskegee, Alabama, Carver saw a land and people in need. His mission became clear — to teach Black farmers how to rejuvenate the soil, grow better crops, and improve their lives. Stepping off the train, he realized that he was the outsider — an educated Northerner in a racially divided community.

Despite facing judgment and prejudice, Carver remained determined to make a difference. He would defy expectations, using his knowledge and passion for uplifting those around him.

Trouble at Tuskegee

George Carver had big responsibilities at Tuskegee. In 1896, he was in charge of the agriculture department, which had only 13 students at the time. But soon, he had a long list of other jobs. He had to manage two farms, an orchard, beehives, and a dairy barn. On top of that, he had to take care of the animals as a vet, keep the school grounds looking good, and oversee the toilets to prevent diseases.

Every day was packed for Carver. He woke up at 4:00 a.m. to take a walk in nature, a routine that refreshed him. Then, he had breakfast with students and started teaching. His schedule was tight, moving from teaching agriculture to art to farmers' classes. In the afternoon, he checked other classes, tested seeds, checked on farm animals, and even inspected cows. Evenings were filled with answering letters and memos from Principal Washington.

Despite his busy schedule, Carver complained about some things. He felt that Washington was micromanaging him too much. He wanted more control over decisions about animals and crops but wasn't allowed. He wrote long letters to Washington, asking for more freedom to do what he knew was right.

At Tuskegee, students were taught practical skills. They made clothes and furniture and even helped build dormitories and classrooms. Carver's early lab equipment was salvaged from the dump because Washington wouldn't buy new items. Carver turned this into a lesson for his chemistry students, teaching them to see the potential in discarded items.

Teaching came naturally to Carver. He used simple language and hands-on activities to help his students understand. He also took them outdoors to observe nature because he believed that education should also happen outside the classroom. Carver didn't dress or teach like a typical teacher, but his methods worked. He encouraged his students to think for themselves and explore their curiosity.

Carver's teaching style reflected his belief that everything in nature is connected. He thought it was essential to understand how plants, animals, and the environment interacted. So, in his botany classes, he didn't just stick to plants. He included bits of history, geography, chemistry, art, and even poetry. Over time, he expanded the courses to include animal nutrition, weather studies, and the study of bacteria.

Carver knew that farming required a lot of knowledge and intelligence.

Unlike other colleges where agricultural classes were mostly for men, Tuskegee welcomed women. They learned various skills like gardening, raising poultry, growing fruits, taking care of dairy animals, and beekeeping. Carver was strict in his teaching, but his students adored him. Despite his unusual voice, it was his kindness and passion for the subject that made him popular among students. He always had time to offer encouragement or advice, which made him stand out as a teacher.

Even students who weren't in Carver's classes sought his company. They were drawn to his wisdom and curiosity about the world. Carver encouraged his students to observe and appreciate the beauty around them. He believed that understanding nature was essential, and he shared this message not only in his classes but also in Bible studies and nature programs for children.

Agricultural Experiment Station

In 1897, just four months after arriving in Tuskegee, Carver was given another responsibility: overseeing the new agricultural experiment station. Despite his already full schedule, Carver was thrilled. He saw this as an opportunity to conduct research that could benefit the local community. Unlike other research centers that focused on high-tech solutions, Carver insisted on using basic tools that tenant farmers could afford, like a hoe, a shovel, or a mule-drawn plow. He wanted every operation at the Tuskegee station to be accessible to the average farmer, helping those with limited resources improve their farming practices.

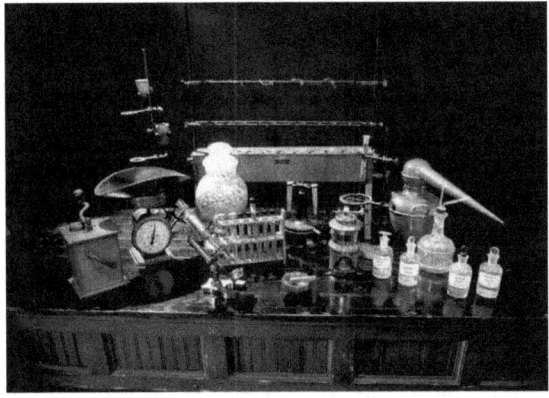

Carver's laboratory equipment.
https://commons.wikimedia.org/wiki/File:George_Washington_Carver-laboratory_equipment.jpeg

Carver faced a significant challenge when he set up the experiment station on 10 acres of poor, eroded land that had been depleted by decades of cotton farming. He saw this as an opportunity to demonstrate proper farming methods. The first task was to improve the soil, which was sandy, gravelly, and prone to erosion due to years of neglect.

Carver believed that the condition of the soil reflected the economic, spiritual, and intellectual well-being of the people who worked it. He considered caring for the soil a moral duty. While commercial fertilizers were recommended, Carver knew most Black sharecroppers couldn't afford them. Instead, he advocated for using organic materials like pine tops, hay, bark, and old cotton stalks to enrich the soil. He encouraged his students to fill eroded gullies with organic matter, promoting soil health and fertility.

By understanding plants' nutritional needs, Carver emphasized the importance of nitrogen, phosphorus, and potassium in soil fertility. He started a compost pile on campus, where organic waste from the kitchen and yard was collected and turned into nutrient-rich compost. Additionally, Carver advocated for the consumption of wild vegetables, which provided both food and medicine. He drew upon his childhood experience of eating weeds and encouraged farmers to collect acorns for animal feed or flour production.

Carver's approach to soil improvement and plant nutrition was rooted in practicality and sustainability. He believed in working with nature rather than against it, utilizing readily available resources to enhance soil fertility and promote agricultural productivity. Through his efforts at the experiment station, Carver aimed to empower farmers with the knowledge and techniques needed to revitalize their land and improve their livelihoods.

Despite the dominance of cotton in the South, Principal Washington urged Carver to continue studying it. Carver, however, also explored other crops, including cowpeas, clover, and soybeans, which enriched the soil and served as valuable livestock feed. Among these, cowpeas stood out for their versatility, being used not only as green manure but also as a nutritious ingredient in various dishes like soups and stews.

In addition to cowpeas, Carver delved into the study of peanuts and sweet potatoes. His interest in sweet potatoes lasted several years, during which he examined their nutritional value and optimal cultivation methods. This research was groundbreaking, as the understanding of nutrition was still in its infancy during the early 20th century. Carver's experiments revealed valuable insights, such as the high protein content in sweet potato vines, which he advocated for feeding to livestock to enhance muscle development.

Despite the loss of many of his research notes, Carver's findings were extensively documented in easy-to-read bulletins, providing valuable insights into the conditions and results of his experiments. He dedicated a significant portion of his publications to the sweet potato, underscoring its importance in his agricultural research endeavors. Through his studies and publications, Carver contributed significantly to the understanding and utilization of various crops, particularly the sweet potato, in agricultural practices.

Carver's dedication to promoting agricultural innovation extended beyond research to practical applications and education. He recognized the importance of household usage of farm products and included recipes in his bulletins, emphasizing the significance of using farm produce wisely and economically. Some recipes were his own creations, while others were sourced from various places. To test these recipes, he sought the assistance of Mrs. Wolcott and her daughters, who provided valuable feedback and adjustments.

Moreover, Carver actively sought to create new markets for crops like peanuts, realizing that encouraging farmers to grow new crops wasn't enough without a corresponding demand. He believed in the untapped potential of every plant and tirelessly explored innovative uses for them.

Additionally, Carver advocated for locally-grown produce as a means to improve nutrition and economic sustainability. He encouraged farmers to diversify their crops beyond cotton, urging them to cultivate vegetable gardens and raise livestock alongside their main crops.

Carver's innovative spirit led him to explore various products derived from peanuts, utilizing all parts of the plant for purposes ranging from face lotion and soap to dyes and rubber. His laboratory experiments showcased the vast potential of agricultural products beyond their traditional uses.

Furthermore, Carver was committed to disseminating agricultural knowledge to farmers. He expanded on Washington's initiatives by organizing monthly Farmers' Institutes, where he provided practical advice and demonstrations on farming techniques. Despite challenges in reaching rural communities, Carver's efforts to engage with people directly through weekend demonstrations and the creation of a movable school known as the Jesup Wagon helped spread agricultural knowledge far and wide.

Ultimately, Carver's tireless dedication to agricultural research, education, and outreach left a lasting impact – not only on the agricultural landscape but also on the lives of countless farmers and communities. His legacy continues to inspire innovation and sustainability in agriculture to this day.

Creative Spirit

Carver's curiosity and creativity extended to the creation of paints from clay. Since his childhood on the Carver farm, he had been experimenting with natural pigments, extracting colors from berries and nuts. While inspecting cows one day, he noticed the clay beneath his feet and decided to investigate further. He brought samples back to his lab and boiled and strained the clay, developing an inexpensive paint for local farmers. Macon County's soil offered a diverse range of colors, from white to yellow to red, allowing for various paint combinations. By adding bluing to white clay, Carver even created a royal blue reminiscent of ancient Egyptian paint. He hoped these paints would enhance the farmer's surroundings, making them healthier, more cheerful, and more beautiful.

Carver showcased his paint samples at fairs and conferences, drawing interest from several paint companies. Despite this, he wasn't keen on commercializing his formulas, as he was already immersed in other projects or preparing for speaking engagements. Carver's lectures became popular forms of entertainment, attracting invitations from various places. While descriptions in newspapers could convey the variety of wood stains and paints he developed, seeing the vibrant royal blue firsthand captivated audiences. Carver dedicated weeks to creating interactive exhibits and providing clear instructions for others to replicate his methods.

Despite skepticism from some at the institute, Carver's innovative ideas found a receptive audience. Apart from Principal Washington, nobody lectured off-campus more than Carver, further spreading his ideas and expertise.

More Responsibilities

On November 14, 1915, Booker T. Washington passed away, leaving George Washington Carver with a mix of memories, including regrets about the disagreements they had. Despite their differences, Carver deeply respected Washington's commitment to uplifting people through education. With Robert Russa Moton taking over as principal of Tuskegee, Carver found more freedom in his research endeavors. Moton recognized Carver's growing fame and reduced his teaching load, encouraging him to take on more speaking engagements.

As Carver's influence expanded nationally and internationally, he received invitations from various organizations, including traditionally white ones. Each speaking engagement required meticulous planning due to the challenges of travel as a Black man in the racially-segregated South. Despite facing discrimination and often being underestimated due to his appearance, Carver remained true to himself, preferring his comfortable, old clothes over newer attire suggested by the college.

World War I brought new challenges and opportunities for Carver. With the United States facing shortages of vital supplies due to disrupted trade routes, Carver's expertise became invaluable. He contributed to wartime conservation efforts by exploring alternatives to imported commodities, such as rubber substitutes from sweet potatoes and clay pigments. Carver's innovative bread-making techniques using wheat and sweet potato flour garnered attention from government officials, earning him respect and recognition.

During a time of economic hardship, Carver emphasized the importance of conservation and resourcefulness. He taught communities how to repurpose waste materials and preserve food through canning, pickling, and drying. Carver's message of abundance in frugality resonated with many during the war years, highlighting the untapped potential in everyday resources.

Carver's contributions were widely recognized. Henry Ford hailed him as the world's greatest living scientist, and Life magazine named him one of the great scientists of the U.S.

When Carver passed away in 1943, President Franklin D. Roosevelt mourned the loss, acknowledging Carver's immense contributions to science and agriculture. Carver's legacy lives on through his numerous publications, his work with farmers, and his collaborations with industry leaders like Henry Ford.

Carver's generosity extended even after his death. He established the George Washington Carver Foundation and left a significant portion of his savings to the Tuskegee Institute, ensuring that his mission of advancing knowledge about plants would continue to benefit future generations.

Chapter 9: Voice of Change: Martin Luther King Jr.'s Dream for Equality

History is filled with many influential characters, but only a few have had a powerful impact, such as Dr. Martin Luther King. He was born during challenging times when African Americans had reached their limits. They were frustrated and angry, ready to erupt like a volcano, destroying everything in their path.

Martin Luther King
https://commons.wikimedia.org/wiki/File:Martin-Luther-King-1964-leaning-on-a-lectern.jpg

Martin Luther King could see that his people had enough. He believed that violence would only bring more violence, and he hoped for a peaceful approach. He showed the world that the oppressed could demand their rights and freedom without shedding a drop of blood. His peaceful approach made him a role model and a hero, and people will continue telling his story for centuries.

This chapter takes you on a journey to the past, where you will meet a legendary African American hero and witness how he made history.

Social and Political Climate

King was born on January 15, 1929. This was a long time ago, so it is easy to imagine that life was different back then. Although people dressed and talked differently, and technology wasn't as prevalent as it is today, the political climate was quite similar. Civil rights activists were accused of being unpatriotic, unAmerican, or communists. These accusations resemble those that the Black Lives Matter movement constantly deals with in the 21st century.

African Americans were subjected to racism, poverty, and violent attacks. The political landscape was unstable, with only a few trying to change things for a better future. Social justice and civil rights movements were spreading across the country and other places worldwide, screaming to a deaf world that Black people had equal rights.

On the other hand, anti-democratic groups and other forces were happy with the status quo and resisted any change that threatened their ignorant views.

King wanted to rise above the bigotry and create what he called a "Beloved Community." He imagined a world without poverty, violence, wars, and racism. His vision inspired peace and civil rights activists who believed it was possible to create that community.

These groups advocated for eradicating outdated and ignorant policing, incarceration, and punishment systems that favored white people. They called for equal rights in health, education, and voting in white communities with Black residents.

Black people didn't fight alone. There were a few white individuals who sided with them and put in time, money, and resources to bring equality to a broken society.

However, King wasn't pleased with the role white allies played, saying on several occasions that he was disappointed as he expected more from them.

He called these individuals "White moderates" and believed that they were the biggest obstacles on the freedom path. They were more concerned with order rather than justice. He accused them of playing a passive role as they didn't call for freedom. They only cared about reducing the tension between Black and white people to create a "false peace." They wanted both sides to appear to get along without granting African Americans any of their rights.

In 1964 and 1965, the government passed the Civil Rights Act and the Voting Rights Act, respectively, but they weren't widely accepted. White people viewed them as controversial, and they led to decades of protests that the conservatives called riots, while the civil rights movement called them revolts. Whether rights or revolts, King believed that they were "the language of the unheard." They caused further division between Black and white people.

Although things often seemed bleak, King was an optimist. He believed that Black people were powerful enough to make history and create an equal society. He spoke of his hopes in the letters he wrote when he was in Birmingham jail.

"We will reach the goal of freedom in Birmingham and all over the nation because the goal of America is freedom."

Early Life

King was born in Atlanta, Georgia, under the name Michael Luther King Jr., to Alberta Williams King and pastor Michael Luther King Sr. When Michael was five years old, his father visited Germany, where he learned about Protestant Reformation leader Martin Luther and his rich history. He was very impressed by everything Martin had achieved and considered him a role model. When he returned home, he changed his and his son's names to Martin.

King had one younger brother, Alfred, and an older sister, Willie. He and his siblings grew up in a loving home with caring and supportive parents. Martin Sr. was strict, but Alberta was sweet and gentle.

In the comfort of his home, King felt safe with his religious and honorable parents. They tried to protect him and his siblings from racism, but they couldn't keep them locked in the house or shield them from their ugly reality.

Martin Sr. influenced his son's activism and fight against racism. He was a man of God and believed that segregation and racism were an insult to his faith. He fought racial prejudice and taught his children to treat everyone with respect. He warned them against acting superior toward those less fortunate than them. These lessons had a huge impact on King.

However, King didn't share his parent's views about religion. He often questioned his faith and expressed discomfort in praying and other aspects of worship.

King was a brilliant and an exceptional student. He attended Booker T. Washington High School and skipped the seventh and ninth grades. In 1944, when he was only 15 years old, he enrolled at Morehouse College. He was very popular, especially with the girls.

During his first two years, King wasn't motivated and had no interest in studying or attending his classes. However, things changed when he started showing an interest in politics. As he grew up, King saw the impact of ignorance and racism on the Black community. He realized that he couldn't just stand and watch injustice prevail. At Morehouse College, he started taking the first steps toward a future in social activism.

He said in his autobiography, *"I could envision myself playing a part in breaking down the legal barriers to Negro rights."* His purpose became clear. To help others, he could have either been a doctor or a lawyer. His father wasn't pleased with his career choice because he wanted him to follow in his and his grandfather's footsteps and join the ministry.

However, in junior year, he changed his mind after taking a Bible class and renewing his faith. He decided to join the church, a decision that pleased his father. In 1948, he was ordained at Ebenezer Baptist Church.

At the age of 19, King graduated from Morehouse College with a sociology degree. Then, he attended Crozer Theological Seminary. He excelled in all his classes and was his class's valedictorian. In 1951, he graduated with a divinity degree, and in 1955, he earned a Ph.D. in systematic theology from Boston University.

Influences and Nonviolence Resistance

During his senior year at Morehouse College, King developed a close relationship with its president, Benjamin E. Mays. Mays was an advocate for equality and believed that religion was the only power that could bring social change. His views influenced King, who considered Mays a role model.

Literature also impacted King's views and nonviolence philosophy. When he was at Morehouse, he read *On the Duty of Civil Disobedience*, an essay by American philosopher Henry David Thoreau. This groundbreaking, albeit controversial essay argues that a person's belief in what's right is more significant than the government's unjust laws.

In 1963, King wrote a letter from Birmingham City Jail that showed the impact of Thoreau's words on his views.

"There are just laws, and there are unjust laws. I would be the first to advocate obeying just laws. One has not only a legal but a moral responsibility to obey just laws. Conversely, one has a moral responsibility to disobey unjust laws. Any law that uplifts human personality is just."

King was most likely talking about the Jim Crow laws, which denied African Americans rights to education, holding jobs, and voting. Any Black person who broke these laws was arrested, fined, sent to jail, or killed.

King believed it was immoral to follow unjust laws and one should take a stand against them. He called for nonviolent resistance with peaceful protests, marches, and sit-ins to create a crisis and push the government to sit and negotiate with them.

King also found inspiration in Gandhi, whose views and words were similar to those of Jesus. However, King didn't accept Gandhi's teachings right away. He found concepts of love and nonviolence unrealistic in a war against oppression. He believed that Jesus's peaceful teaching could only work with personal relationships – and not to change laws.

"I came to see for the first time that the Christian doctrine of love operating through the Gandhian method of nonviolence was one of the most potent weapons available to oppressed people in their struggle for freedom."

He agreed with Gandhi that the most powerful weapons oppressed people had were love and truth in their fight for justice and freedom.

King knew that many people would be skeptical about the notion of nonviolence. He often explained in his letters and autobiography that love was powerful enough to bring real change.

"Love for Gandhi was a potent instrument for social and collective transformation. It was in this Gandhian emphasis on love and nonviolence that I discovered the method for social reform that I had been seeking."

To help people better understand his views, he created six principles for nonviolence.

1. *"Nonviolence is a way of life for courageous people."*
2. *"Nonviolence seeks to win friendship and understanding."*
3. *"Nonviolence seeks to defeat injustice, not people."*
4. *"Nonviolence holds that suffering for a just cause can educate and transform."*
5. *"Nonviolence chooses love instead of hate."*
6. *"Nonviolence believes that the universe is on the side of justice."*

Civil Rights Activism

King became the voice of the oppressed. He called for equality and freedom while advocating for upholding a nonviolent philosophy and religious beliefs. He became a civil rights leader, and soon, he faced his biggest tests.

In 1955, a 15-year-old Black girl called Claudette Colvin broke the Jim Crow laws by refusing to give up her bus seat to a white man. King wanted to take advantage of this incident to challenge these laws. However, Colvin was young and pregnant, so he decided against it since it would attract negative press.

A few months later, the legendary Rosa Parks incident occurred, leading to the Montgomery Bus Boycott. Local civil rights leaders found King the perfect person to lead the boycott because he was well-trained, charismatic, and young, so African Americans were more likely to listen to him.

"We have no alternative but to protest. For many years, we have shown an amazing patience. We have sometimes given our white brothers the feeling that we liked the way we were being treated. But we come here tonight to be saved from that patience that makes us patient with anything less than freedom and justice."

His speech was powerful and moving. Using words like "our white brothers" sent a clear message of love and peace. It reminded the Black community that they were all brothers looking to coexist.

King's role in the boycott caused him many problems. He faced multiple death threats, was arrested, and his home was set on fire. After the boycott, King became a national hero and the voice of the civil rights movement.

In 1960, a group of Black students in South Carolina defied the Jim Crow laws by sitting at white people's lunch counters. They were told to leave and sit in the "colored" section, but they refused. When the news reached King, he applauded the students for using nonviolent methods.

In 1960, 27 cities ended the lunch segregation law. Although that was a big step, King knew they still had a long way to go.

A few months later, King went to a department store with 75 students and requested to be seated at a lunch counter. The store refused to serve them and asked them to leave. However, King and the boys sat in to protest. King and 36 of the students were arrested that day. However, they were released soon after as Atlanta's mayor was worried that arresting dozens of Black men would attract negative press.

In 1963, civil rights activists Bayard Rustin, A. Philip Randolph, and King organized a massive march in Washington, asking to change segregation laws. Two hundred fifty thousand people participated in the march, making it one of the largest demonstrations the country had ever seen.

During that march, King delivered one of the most famous and inspiring speeches in history.

"I have a dream that one day, on the red hills of Georgia, the sons of former slaves and the sons of former slave owners will be able to sit down together at the table of brotherhood. I have a dream that my four little children will one day live in a nation where they will not be judged by the color of their skin but by the content of their character. I have a dream today."

King's *"I Have a Dream"* speech was simple yet powerful. He again reminded them that white and Black people were brothers and should live together in peace. He wanted his children to grow up in a tolerant world where they would be judged for their character rather than their skin color.

The movement and the speech had a huge impact on American society. Many white people across the country started to question the treatment of African Americans and the Jim Crow laws. In 1964, the government outlawed discrimination in public facilities.

After the huge success of the Washington march, civil rights activists Hosea Williams and John Lewis set out on another one in 1965, in Selma, demanding equal voting rights. However, the police met demonstrators with tear gas and nightsticks. What started as a peaceful march turned into a violent attack, with 58 people hospitalized. It was one of the bloodiest days in American history, and people across the country saw images and videos of police brutality against peaceful demonstrators.

King wasn't present in the Selma march. On March 9, 1965, another one took place, and King was present. 2,500 Black and white Americans participated. To avoid confrontation, King asked his followers to kneel in prayer. Two other marches took place in the same month. The second one saw 25,000 people marching in peace and King delivering another powerful peace. Five months later, African Americans were granted the right to vote.

Friendship with Lyndon Baines Johnson

Former president Lyndon Baines Johnson and King shared a close bond. However, this partnership took place behind closed doors since their advisors didn't completely trust each other. Yet, both men fully supported one another. Johnson approved the Voting Rights Act and the Civil Rights Act, which ended legal segregation. He referred to them as his administration's biggest accomplishments.

Although many people in the Senate were against passing the Civil Rights Act, Johnson created the first-ever bipartisan coalition to challenge and overcome their filibuster.

In 1964, King publicly supported Johnson during the presidential campaign, which garnered him a large share of the votes.

Martin Luther King and Malcolm X

Although King and Malcolm had the same goals and met the same fate, both men were more adversaries than allies. They only met once, and their conversation lasted a minute. A Black-and-white picture is all that remains of this historic moment, reminding people of what could have been.

King and Malcolm didn't agree on many issues. Malcolm disagreed with King's nonviolent approach, finding it weak and slow, while King didn't appreciate Malcolm advocating for self-defense.

King once described him as very articulate, but he disagreed with his philosophical and political views, while Malcolm described him as a "modern Uncle Tom."

However, Malcolm sent a letter to King as an olive branch, asking him to put their minor differences aside and focus on their common goals. He invited King to join a Harlem rally but didn't attend.

Malcolm, however, attended the Washinton march and called it a farce and a circus. He also criticized King's *I Have a Dream* speech.

When Malcolm was assassinated, King mourned him, saying that the world lost a great leader. He also sent Malcolm's widow a telegram to express his sympathies.

"While we did not always see eye to eye on methods to solve the race problem, I always had a deep affection for Malcolm and felt that he had a great ability to put his finger on the existence and root of the problem."

One can't help but wonder what would have happened had these men lived longer and mended their relationship.

On April 4, 1968, three years after Malcolm's assassination, King was also assassinated. Both men were 39 years old.

Martin Luther's King's Legacy

The political and social climate hasn't changed much in the last hundred years. American society is still divided, and Black people are still calling out against injustice. As a result, King's teachings remain as relevant today as they were 80 years ago. Black activists still call out against police brutality and discrimination. Many still echo King's *I Have a Dream* speech, hoping for the day they would be judged for their character rather than their skin color.

They still repeat King's message, asking for environmental justice, equal education, and voting rights.

After George Floyd's death, many Americans applied King's nonviolence philosophy. They held sit-ins or marched peacefully. In 2023, King's son and other civil rights activists held a rally in Washington to commemorate the 60th anniversary of King's famous march.

In 2011, Egyptians held nonviolent marches in Egypt demanding President Mubarak to resign. In Hiroshima, Japan, the people celebrate his birthday every year and recall his messages of peace. In Poland, a social movement used nonviolent resistance to call for worker rights.

King has become an image of freedom and peaceful resistance worldwide. He is still the voice of the oppressed, and many resonate with his philosophy. The *"I Have a Dream"* Speech has become an empowering message of hope.

Martin Luther King died, but his messages are universal and eternal.

Chapter 10: Trailblazer in the Sky: Bessie Coleman's Aviation Adventures

In a time where sexism, racism, and blatant disrespect for others based on blind bigotry went unchecked, one female pilot of Black and native descent decided to break new ground and soar through the clouds, searching for glory and immortality. Brave Bessie, as some called her, was the first woman in the field of aviation to fight against and break the chains engineered by the white patriarchy to dampen the dreams of all those who were deemed different by the men in power.

Her courageous endeavors and perseverance continue to this day to inspire generations to set their sights on the impossible and turn it into something probable.

During Coleman's time, it wasn't abnormal to observe children of darker skin tones working in challenging conditions, like picking cotton in the scorching sun. It also wasn't unusual for those same children to be subjected to harassment and discrimination within their society from the people who considered themselves of a higher status.

Black Americans at the time had no right to vote, ride in railway cars with their white counterparts, or even have the same chance to acquire a proper education as those with fairer skin.

So, who exactly was Bessie Coleman, and how did she acquire such renown and respect considering her circumstances?

Early Life

Young Bessie was born on the 26th of January 1892 in hot Atlanta, Texas. Her parents were Susan Coleman, an African American, and George Coleman, who was a mix of African American and Native American bloodlines. Bessie was the 10th child in a household with 13 siblings, making it hard for her parents to provide for them while working as a maid and a sharecropper picking cotton for a landowner.

When she was six years old, Coleman attended a segregated school in Waxahachie, Texas. At the time, people of color were not allowed to attend school with white children. The school was described as a one-room wooden shack – with very little chance of having proper school supplies provided, such as paper and pencils. It would take little Bessie a four-mile walk every day to get to the makeshift school, which was a far cry from where the white children attended.

No sooner after that, in 1901, her father decided to abandon his paternal duties and head on to Oklahoma in an effort to escape the brutal discrimination and perhaps reconnect with his native roots. Her mother remained in Texas with her and her siblings, doing her best to provide for them using what small wages she could acquire. She was used to working odd jobs, like picking cotton and washing laundry. As soon as they were old enough and able, Bessie and her siblings headed out into the world to find jobs to help their mother out with the household expenses. One of the jobs that Bessie participated in was picking cotton when it was ripe... something she truly hated doing.

In 1910, Bessie joined the Oklahoma Colored Agricultural and Normal University (currently known as Langston University); however, she had to drop out given that she didn't have enough funds to cover the school fees.

In 1915, when she was 23 and during the great migration, Coleman set out to Chicago, Illinois, and secured living arrangements with two of her brothers while attending the Burnham School of Beauty Culture. She then went on to work as a manicurist in a barber shop on the south side of the city. It is speculated that she got married on January 30th, 1917, to Claude Glenn – a man 14 years older than her. Her brothers served in the military during WWI, and when they returned, they had a stock of stories to tell about their time in France.

Their tales surpassed Bessie's imagination. They spoke of the freedoms the French women enjoyed that she was only allowed to dream about. They told her of how the women of France were to be granted the right to become whatever they wanted, even pilots. Her brother often taunted her, saying that this was something that she would never become. While they were reciting their adventures in France, her brother, John, went on saying, "I know something that French women do that you'll never do... fly!" "That's it... You just called it for me!" was Bessie's response to her brother after setting her mind on walking in the footsteps of the French, becoming a pilot herself, and proving him wrong.

The Road to France

Bessie was not prepared for the backlash she would receive once she decided to enter the field of aviation. The landscape in America at the time didn't exactly advocate for women to enter male-dominated fields, not to mention Black women.

Coleman saved up enough money to apply to the U.S. flight schools and reached out to pilots to teach her flying, but every time she did, she was met with rejection and disdain, being a woman and being Black. Still determined to follow her dream, Coleman sought the advice of her friend, Robert Abbott, who at the time was the publisher of the well-known African American newspaper, *"The Chicago Defender."*

Abbott suggested that the young woman take matters into her own hands, learn French, and head out to France to earn her pilot's license. She was able to secure funding from Abbott for her trip and another generous African American benefactor, Jesse Binga, who founded the first Black-owned Bank in Chicago.

By November 20th, 192o, Bessie had taught herself French, traveled to France, and enrolled in the Caudron Brothers School of Aviation "Le Crotoy," located in Northern France near the Somme. She was the only student with dark skin in her class. On June 15th, 1921, she graduated from the Federation Aeronautique Internationale, becoming the very first African American woman to earn a pilot's license within seven months only.

The training was focused on flying the Nieuport type 82. Due to the brittle state of the plane, it was customary for Bessie to inspect every last part of it before take-off, just in case. The plane consisted of two cockpits, one for the instructor and the other for the student. The machine didn't resemble any of its modern counterparts. It had no steering wheel, no brakes, and was mainly managed by a large wooden stick that was in charge of the plane's pitch and roll (rotating the plane around the side-to-side axis and front-to-back axis) and a rudder bar for controlling the yaw (rotating the plane around the vertical axis.)

After this triumph, she felt she needed to learn a little more before venturing into the field of stunt flying on her own.

Bessie continued her journey around Europe, learning the many techniques of stunt flying, like doing loops, tailspins, and banking, among other fascinating stunts. During her lessons, she was present when an unfortunate accident claimed the life of one of the other students.

Bessie recalls the incident, saying, *"It was a terrible shock to my nerves, but I never lost them... I kept going."*

Part of her training included flying with the German military aces during her 10 weeks in Berlin.

The Way Back Home

In September 1922, Coleman returned to the United States as a different woman than when she left. Against all odds, she was now officially a pilot. She was greeted by a swarm of reporters who dubbed her "A full-fledged Aviatrix, the first of her race."

When she was invited to the all-Black musical Shuffle Along, she received a standing ovation from both the audience and the white orchestra. Bessie often dreamed of building a school for aviation to accommodate women of her complexion. So, she began making a name for herself. Her first official appearance was at an American airshow sponsored by Abbott and The Defender. The show honored all Black veterans of the 396th Infantry Regiment who served in World War I, and she was introduced as the world's greatest woman flier.

The Journey to Fame

Her first public flight in the U.S. was on the 3rd of September, 1922. She'd borrowed a Curtiss JN-4D Jenny in Curtiss Field, in Long Island. After that, she headed to Memphis, Tennessee, and then to an exhibit in the Checkerboard field in Chicago on October 15th, where she was met with 2,000 friendly integrated faces.

At the beginning of 1923, she traveled to California for a promotional opportunity in collaboration with Coast Tire and Rubber of Oakland.

The venture was meant to put her on the map as a barnstorming pilot (a form of stunt flying), one of the few jobs available for aviators at the time.

She started touring the United States, performing impossible tricks and unbelievable feats that the Americans had never seen before for the first five years following her return from Europe. She would perform loops, barrel rolls, near-ground dips, and figure eights with her plane. She'd walk on the wings mid-flight while the controls were managed by her co-pilot and then parachute her way to the ground. Many newspapers, especially Black ones, started covering her unusual and spectacular airborne feats. Before long, she was called Queen Bess, and Brave Bessie. Coleman wasn't just interested in having her name carved in the Hall of Fame; she was making a statement.

She was invited to perform in several venues and give speeches in others; however, Coleman followed one simple rule when it came to performing in public – she never went to places that segregated the white and Black crowds. She made sure that the venue she was visiting allowed all the audience to enter through a single gate, not separate ones based on color.

Coleman was given the opportunity to star in a movie based on her own life story. However, she was quick to turn down the opportunity to be on the silver screen after learning that the feature would start with her appearing to wear rags. In an interview with Billboard magazine, she was quoted saying, "No Uncle Tom stuff for me," regarding her stance on the movie.

Surviving Her First Accident

In 1923, only two years into her flight career, Bessie Coleman looked death in the eye and lived to tell the tale. Coleman had been saving money to buy her plane instead of having to borrow them for her performances. She had her eyes set on a military surplus Curtiss JN-4, also known as Jenny. Bessie made her way to Santa Monica, California, to seal the deal.

While in California, she had an airshow planned near Los Angeles. After taking off from the fairgrounds, fate had other plans for her. At a height of 300 feet, her engine stalled, and her plane started to nose-dive toward the ground. She crashed and, in the process, broke her leg, fractured her ribs, and totaled the plane.

She tried to reason with the doctor present at the location of the accident to just patch her up so she could make the show in time. In response to her pleas, the doctor called for an ambulance.

In a telegram directed to her fans, Coleman said, *"Tell them all that as soon as I can walk, I'm going to fly!"*

Her injuries were severe enough that it took months for her to recover, and it wasn't before two years had passed that she was able to fly again regularly.

The incident left a mark on brave Bessie. While she went back to performing shows in Texas, she seemed to be increasing her professional presence in the lecture circuit – a line of work she deemed safer and more rewarding in terms of monetary value while also making a point about the social situation present at the time.

During her speeches, she'd include pictures and feature movies of her flights with the German aviators. These talks would often leave the audiences in awe, especially the female Black population, who would then offer accommodation and meals. These appearances often paid more than flying performances.

The Second Accident – Bessie Coleman's Unfortunate Demise

It was said that at the time, Coleman had almost saved enough money to open her own flying school like she had dreamed. In April of 1926, she'd rounded up enough cash to buy herself another Surplus Jenny instead of the one that crashed and burned in 1923.

On April 30th, Coleman and her co-pilot and mechanic, William Wills, went out for a rehearsal flight for a show that was scheduled on May 1st. Coleman was in the second cockpit unbuckled so she could look over the edge to find a suitable area to land for her parachute jump stunt on the day of the show. In an unfortunate turn-on event, due to a mechanical malfunction that was then attributed to a wrench being stuck in the engine, the plane started acting up. Based on eyewitness records, Wills flew the plane first for about five minutes at an altitude of 2,000 feet. He then climbed up to 3,500 feet. Out of nowhere, the plane suddenly accelerated in speed, made an abrupt nose dive, went into a tailspin, and finally flipped upside down, essentially flinging the unbuckled Coleman from an altitude presumed to be 2,000 feet. Bessie

Coleman plummeted to the ground and passed away upon impact at the age of 34.

Bessie Coleman died only five years after starting her aviation career.

William Wills didn't enjoy a better fortune than Coleman. In fact, some believe he endured a more painful death. The co-pilot crashed with the plane to the ground and was found stuck under the plane's body.

While the rescuers were scrambling to get him out of the wreckage, someone thought it would be a grand idea to light a match for a cigarette. Needless to say, the act set the gas fumes on fire and turned the wreckage into a flaming mess.

Her death barely drew the attention of the mainstream media. In fact, most outlets ignored her tragic departure and instead focused their attention on reporting on William Wills' death, who happened to be white and male.

However, many Black publications honored and mourned the passing of Brave Bessie by dedicating their front page to cover her untimely death.

To honor her passing, Bessie's body was laid in state in both Florida and Chicago so that people could get an opportunity to pay their respects to the late pilot. 10,000 flocked from all over to glance one last time at the formidable woman and say their goodbyes. Journalist Ida B. Wells, who was well known for her public disdain and fight against lynching, was in charge of leading the ceremonies in Chicago.

For several years following her death, planes flew over her grave.

Bessie Colemans's Legacy

In 1929, Bessie Coleman's wish came true, though she wasn't alive to see her dreams come to fruition. The Bessie Coleman Aero Club was formed by African American pilot LT Willian J. Powell.

The Challenger Air Pilots Association started to sponsor annual memorial events as a tribute to the late aviator in the 1930s. These memorials included flying over Bessie Coleman's grave to drop flowers.

Over the years, different authors have recited Bessie Coleman's story in many forms. Her life has been featured in television series, books, French documentaries, and even comedy shows.

It wasn't until recent years that Coleman started getting the recognition she deserved beyond the African American Community. In 1995, a stamp with her image was printed in honor of her memory by the United States Postal Service as part of the Black Heritage series.

In Texas, a middle school and multiple roads around the country are named after the pilot, most of which are close to airports in reference to her career. Several aircraft clubs, scholarships, and manufacturers adopted her name.

In 1992, Mae Jemison, the first African American woman to enter space, paid tribute to the late pilot in an afterword titled *"Queen Bess: Daredevil Aviator."*

She expressed her sadness and embarrassment at not knowing about the famous aviator except when her trip to space seemed to loom around the corner. "I wish I had known her while I was growing up... but then again, I think she was there with me all the time," reminiscent Jemison.

Mae recalled taking a picture of Bessie with her to space, which technically makes her earlier statement true. She was indeed with her the whole time, soaring higher than she had ever imagined possible.

In 2000, Bessie was admitted into the Texas Aviation Hall of Fame. Future Female pilots owe a good portion of their successes to the efforts exerted by the late pilot. Willa Brown and Janet Bragg are among the few pilots who soared in the skies after Bessie paved the way for female African Americans to venture into the previously presumed impossible field to enter.

It is without a doubt that even though she led a short life, Bessie Coleman led a full, eventful, and inspiring existence. Her ventures and courage serve as a reminder to today's youth that just because someone says you can't doesn't mean you shouldn't. Even though her story didn't garner the deserved attention until decades after her passing, it still ignites a sense of whimsy and courage in young people, regardless of their gender, ethnicity, or skin tone.

Conclusion

These heroic stories do not exist for people just to admire them. Their amazing stories can seem unreachable, but they were just as human as anyone on the planet today. They encountered challenges and faced opposition, but they persevered with determination. Their innovative thinking and unmatched leadership caused all the heroes of this book to be permanently stamped into the archives of history.

Reading their stories keeps the memories of their struggles and triumphs alive. Forgetting the contributions of these icons would be a huge loss to the collective memory of the world. People rarely rise to the top of their fields and reshape the world while doing it. It takes a special person with the courage to follow their dreams and construct their vision while caring deeply for others to excel so limitlessly.

Their stories are diverse, but the common threads of overcoming adversity and fighting injustice weave together the beautiful story of Blackness. Through their self-determination and unwavering commitment to their ideals, each of these individuals achieved the unthinkable in often dire circumstances. Each of these individuals mastered the magic of turning their hurdles into trampolines in their unique roles.

From politics and religion to music, literature, and mathematics, the Black story has thousands of unread pages. Africans on the continent and in the diaspora have made an impact on the world by excelling in their fields and transforming minds. Through their example, the world is inspired to trailblaze new frontiers of excellence.

Their memory can be a living one if it is kept breathing through the ideas and actions of people now. Their transformative lives do not need to exist in the shadow of stories but can emerge through the applied efforts of the masses. They were committed to their goals until they passed; now, the mantle has been handed over to the next generation. Where these heroes ran, the heroes of the future will fly.

This is not a tale of the past but a mirror to reflect human potential. These heroes are not out of a fictional account from the imagination of a brilliantly creative writer. Their lives printed their narratives, and this can never be duplicated, but it can be elevated. From the foundations laid by these powerful icons, the world can springboard beyond all limitations.

As humanity progresses into an uncertain future, the giants of the past can become a torch to light the path forward. Many of the struggles that the contemporary world faces are sequels to what these heroes had to overcome. By adopting their blueprint, equality, justice, and positive change in the world will come.

If you enjoyed this book, a review on Amazon would be greatly appreciated because it would mean a lot to hear from you.

To leave a review:
1. Open your camera app.
2. Point your mobile device at the QR code.
3. The review page will appear in your web browser.

_____

Thanks for your support!

Check out another book in the series

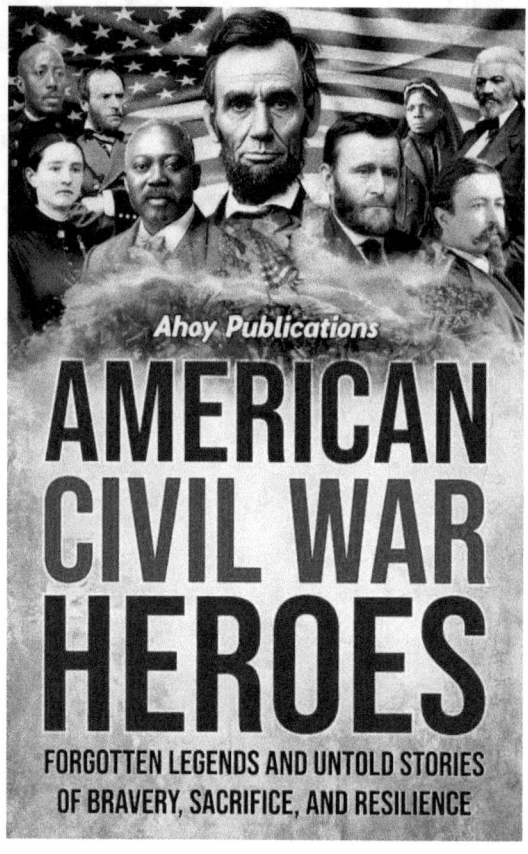

Welcome Aboard, Check Out This Limited-Time Free Bonus!

Ahoy, reader! Welcome to the Ahoy Publications family, and thanks for snagging a copy of this book! Since you've chosen to join us on this journey, we'd like to offer you something special.

Check out the link below for a FREE e-book filled with delightful facts about American History.

But that's not all - you'll also have access to our exclusive email list with even more free e-books and insider knowledge. Well, what are ye waiting for? Click the link below to join and set sail toward exciting adventures in American History.

Access your bonus here

https://ahoypublications.com/

Or, Scan the QR code!

References

11.4 Truth and Reconciliation Commission – The Presidential Years. (n.d.). Tpy.nelsonmandela.org. https://tpy.nelsonmandela.org/pages/part-iv-transformation/11-reconciliation/11-4-truth-and-reconciliation-commission

30 Best Duke Ellington Quotes With Image | Bookey. (n.d.). Www.bookey.app. https://www.bookey.app/quote-author/duke-ellington

A quote from I Know Why the Caged Bird Sings. (n.d.). Www.goodreads.com. https://www.goodreads.com/quotes/9687740-the-act-of-rape-on-an-eight-year-old-body-is-a

Admin. (2022, May 27). 7 Bessie Coleman Fun Facts. Wings over Camarillo. https://wingsovercamarillo.com/7-bessie-coleman-fun-facts/

Adu-Gyamfi, K. (2021). What You Do Not Know about Archbishop Desmond Tutu. Africanews. https://www.africanews.com/2021/12/31/what-you-do-not-know-about-archbishop-desmond-tutu//

Alexander, K. L. (2018). Bessie Coleman. National Women's History Museum. https://www.womenshistory.org/education-resources/biographies/bessie-coleman

Allen. (2015, September 15). Harriet Tubman. History. https://kids.nationalgeographic.com/history/article/harriet-tubman

Anirudh. (2018a, September 11). 10 Major Accomplishments of Rosa Parks | Learnodo Newtonic. Learnodo-Newtonic.com. https://learnodo-newtonic.com/rosa-parks-accomplishments

Archbishop Emeritus Desmond Mpilo Tutu. (2018, May 29). South African History Online. https://www.sahistory.org.za/people/archbishop-emeritus-desmond-mpilo-tutu

Berresford, M. (n.d.). Articles p5. Www.vjm.biz. https://www.vjm.biz/articles4.htm

Bessie Coleman. (n.d.). Airandspace.si.edu. https://airandspace.si.edu/explore/stories/bessie-coleman

Billy Strayhorn and Duke Ellington's Collaboration. (n.d.). Colburn. https://www.colburnschool.edu/community-initiatives/billy-strayhorn/billy-strayhorn-and-duke-ellingtons-collaboration/

Biography.com Editors And Tim Ott. (2024, January 12). Martin Luther King Jr.: Revered Civil Rights Leader. Biography. https://www.biography.com/activists/martin-luther-king-jr#early-life

BrainyQuote. (2017). BrainyQuote; BrainyQuote. https://www.brainyquote.com/authors/katherine-johnson-quotes

Bredhoff, S., Schamel, W., & Potter, L. A. (2016, December 21). An Act of Courage, The Arrest Records of Rosa Parks. National Archives. https://www.archives.gov/education/lessons/rosa-parks

Brown, D. L. (2018, January 14). Martin Luther King Jr. met Malcolm X just once. The photo still haunts us with what was lost. The Washington Post. https://www.washingtonpost.com/news/retropolis/wp/2018/01/14/martin-luther-king-jr-met-malcolm-x-just-once-the-photo-still-haunts-us-with-what-was-lost/

Caplan, A. (2013, December 9). Bioethicist: Mandela's AIDS legacy of silence and courage. NBC News. https://www.nbcnews.com/healthmain/bioethicist-mandelas-aids-legacy-silence-courage-2D11702797

Carver, George Washington. (n.d.). Encyclopedia of Alabama. https://encyclopediaofalabama.org/article/george-washington-carver/

Danielle. (2021, May 5). Harriet Tubman. Harriet Tubman Byway. https://harriettubmanbyway.org/harriet-tubman/

Dawn, R. (2014, May 28). Maya Angelou left lasting pop culture legacy. TODAY.com. https://www.today.com/popculture/maya-angelou-left-lasting-pop-culture-legacy-2D79725094

Dawson, S. (2015). Harriet Tubman. National Women's History Museum; National Women's History Museum. https://www.womenshistory.org/education-resources/biographies/harriet-tubman

Debczak, M. (2018, August 24). 10 Fascinating Facts About Katherine Johnson. Mental Floss. https://www.mentalfloss.com/article/555114/facts-about-katherine-johnson-nasa#_xdp702xtq

Defiance Campaign 1952: The Defiance Campaign in South Africa, recalled – ANC. (n.d.). African National Congress. https://www.anc1912.org.za/defiance-campaign-1952-the-defiance-campaign-in-south-africa-recalled/

Dersch, A. (2024, February 5). Bessie Coleman: A Pioneer in Aviation and Equality. Evergreen Museum. https://www.evergreenmuseum.org/2024/02/05/bessie-coleman-a-pioneer-in-aviation-and-equality/

Desmond Tutu. (n.d.). Theelders.org. https://theelders.org/profile/desmond-tutu

Duke Ellington and his Cotton Club Orchestra - The Syncopated Times. (2020, April 9). The Syncopated Times. https://syncopatedtimes.com/duke-ellington-and-his-cotton-club-orchestra/

Dunbar, E. A. (2019, November 1). The True Story of Harriet Tubman Shows That Sometimes Running Is as Brave as Fighting. Time. https://time.com/5715477/harriet-tubman-escape/

Ellis, E. (2024, January 26). Happy birthday, Bessie Coleman! Science Museum Blog. https://blog.sciencemuseum.org.uk/happy-birthday-bessie-coleman/

Fleur, N. St. (2021, January 28). George Washington Carver. History. https://kids.nationalgeographic.com/history/article/george-washington-carver

George Washington Carver. (n.d.). Science History Institute. https://www.sciencehistory.org/education/scientific-biographies/george-washington-carver/

Giberson, L. (n.d.). Maya Angelou: Finding a Voice through her Complex Vision of Self and Shakespeare. https://dialogues.rutgers.edu/journals/95-maya-angelou-finding-a-voice-through-her-complex-vision-of-self-and-shakespeare/file

Green, K. (2022, February 7). 45 Quotes From the Underground Railroad Operator and Future Face of the $20 Bill, Harriet Tubman. Parade: Entertainment, Recipes, Health, Life, Holidays. https://parade.com/1331514/kaigreen/harriet-tubman-quotes/

Harriet Tubman (U.S. National Park Service). (2023, January 6). Nps.gov; National Park Service. https://www.nps.gov/people/harriet-tubman.htm

Harriet Tubman. (2009, October 29). History.com; A&E Television Networks. https://www.history.com/topics/black-history/harriet-tubman

Harrison, J. (2019, April 5). Women in tech history: Katherine Johnson, the mathematician who guided us to the moon. Medium. https://geneticjen.medium.com/women-in-tech-history-katherine-johnson-the-mathematician-who-guided-us-to-the-moon-6cc54160aedc

History.com Editors. (2018, February 28). Jim Crow Laws. History; A&E Television Networks. https://www.history.com/topics/early-20th-century-us/jim-crow-laws

History.com Editors. (2019, January 7). George Washington Carver. History.com; A&E Television Networks. https://www.history.com/topics/black-history/george-washington-carver

How did Rosa Parks help the NAACP? – idswater.com. (2020, September 11). Ids-Water.com. https://ids-water.com/2020/09/11/how-did-rosa-parks-help-the-naacp/

International, L. on E. / W. M. F. / P. R. (n.d.). Living on Earth: One Step Further: The Story of Katherine Johnson. Living on Earth. https://www.loe.org/shows/segments.html?programID=24-P13-00008&segmentID=2

Joseph, P. (2023, January 16). Commentary: Political, Social Climate of Martin Luther King Jr.'s Era Not So Different from Today's. Texas Standard. https://www.texasstandard.org/stories/commentary-mlk-day-2023/

Kelly, D. (2020, June 10). The /Untold Truth of Rosa Parks. Grunge. https://www.grunge.com/216734/the-untold-truth-of-rosa-parks/

Kennedy, D. (2019, August 13). The Untold Truth Of Harriet Tubman. Grunge. https://www.grunge.com/161879/the-untold-truth-of-harriet-tubman/

Kitazawa, E. (2022, December 17). Racism in the Segregated South: John Griffin's Account. Shortform Books. https://www.shortform.com/blog/racism-in-the-south/

Krasny, J. (2014, May 28). The Creative Habits That Sparked Maya Angelou's Greatest Work. Inc.com. https://www.inc.com/jill-krasny/maya-angelou-creative-writing-process.html

Lauria-Blum, J. (2019, June 7). Bessie Coleman. Www.cradleofaviation.org. https://www.cradleofaviation.org/history/history/women-in-aviation/bessie-coleman.html

Lawrence, A. H. (2001). Duke Ellington and His World. Archive.nytimes.com. https://archive.nytimes.com/www.nytimes.com/books/first/l/lawrence-ellington.html

Life Story: Katherine Johnson. (n.d.). Women & the American Story. https://wams.nyhistory.org/growth-and-turmoil/cold-war-beginnings/katherine-johnson/

Little, B. (2021, January 19). How Martin Luther King Jr. Took Inspiration From Gandhi on Nonviolence. Biography. https://www.biography.com/activists/martin-luther-king-jr-gandhi-nonviolence-inspiration

Makow, H. (2017). Rosa Parks - Why Do Americans Worship Traitors? HenryMakow.com. https://www.henrymakow.com/Rosa-Parks-Proof-Communists.html

Margaritoff, M. (2019, October 26). Beyond The Underground Railroad: Harriet Tubman's Journey From Slave To Spy To Historical Icon. All That's Interesting; All That's Interesting. https://allthatsinteresting.com/harriet-tubman

Martínez, A. (2023, April 4). Maya Angelou, An Essential Voice in American Literature and Culture. EL PAÍS English. https://english.elpais.com/culture/2023-04-04/maya-angelou-an-essential-voice-in-american-literature-and-culture.html

Maya Angelou. (n.d.). Academy of Achievement. https://achievement.org/achiever/maya-angelou

McEvoy, C. (2021, March 26). Rosa Parks - Quotes, Bus Boycott & Death. Biography; A&E Television Networks. https://www.biography.com/activists/rosa-parks

McKnight, M. (2020, July 20). Nelson Mandela's Childhood. The Borgen Project. https://borgenproject.org/nelson-mandelas-childhood-2/

Missouri Department of Agriculture. (n.d.). George Washington Carver. Agriculture.mo.gov. https://agriculture.mo.gov/gwc.php

MLK's Influence. (n.d.). Margmayangelou.weebly.com. https://margmayangelou.weebly.com/mlks-influence.html

Mobayed, T. (2019, February 21). The Sad, Unknown Stories About Malcolm X and His Relationship With Muhammad Ali and Maya Angelou. MVSLIM. https://mvslim.com/the-sad-unknown-stories-about-malcolm-x-and-his-relationship-with-muhammad-ali-and-maya-angelou/

Mullenweg, M. (n.d.). Compendium of Jazz Quotes – Duke Ellington – Jason Heath's Double Bass Blog. Jason Heath's Double Bass Blog. https://doublebassblog.org/2008/02/compendium-of-jazz-quotes-duke-ellington.html

NAACP. (2022). Rosa Parks | NAACP. Naacp.org; NAACP. https://naacp.org/find-resources/history-explained/civil-rights-leaders/rosa-parks

National Geographic Staff. (2023, January 12). Martin Luther King, Jr.—facts and information. National Geographic. https://www.nationalgeographic.com/culture/article/martin-luther-king-jr

National Park Service. (2021, February 15). Lyndon B Johnson's Relationship with MLK - George Washington Memorial Parkway (U.S. National Park Service). Www.nps.gov. https://www.nps.gov/gwmp/learn/historyculture/lbjandmlk.htm

National Women's Hall Of Fame. (2018). Coleman, Bessie - National Women's Hall of Fame. National Women's Hall of Fame. https://www.womenofthehall.org/inductee/bessie-coleman/

Nelson Mandela Foundation. (n.d.). Biography of Nelson Mandela – Nelson Mandela Foundation. Www.nelsonmandela.org. https://www.nelsonmandela.org/biography

Npr. (2023, January 16). "I Have a Dream" Speech, in Its Entirety. Npr.org; Npr. https://www.npr.org/2010/01/18/122701268/i-have-a-dream-speech-in-its-entirety

On The Pulse Of Morning by Maya Angelou. (n.d.). Allpoetry.com. https://allpoetry.com/On-The-Pulse-Of-Morning

PBS. (2002, December 12). Duke Ellington | About Duke Ellington | American Masters | PBS. American Masters; PBS. https://www.pbs.org/wnet/americanmasters/duke-ellington-about-duke-ellington/586/

PBS. (2019). Bessie Coleman | American Experience | PBS. Pbs.org. https://www.pbs.org/wgbh/americanexperience/features/flygirls-bessie-coleman/

Piccotti, T. (2014, April 3). Harriet Tubman - Movie, Quotes & 20 Dollar Bill. Biography; A&E; Television Networks. https://www.biography.com/activists/harriet-tubman

Piccotti, T. (2021, May 10). Maya Angelou: Beloved American Author and Activist. Biography. https://www.biography.com/authors-writers/maya-angelou#early-life

Rise, S. I. (n.d.). Still, I Rise by Maya Angelou. Allpoetry.com. https://allpoetry.com/poem/8511437-Still-I-Rise-by-Maya-Angelou

Rosa Parks: Timeline of Her Life, Montgomery Bus Boycott and Death. (2023, October 29). Hec.edu.vn - Useful Knowledge Information. https://hec.edu.vn/rosa-parks-timeline-of-her-life-montgomery-bus-boycott-and-death/

Rosenberg, J. (2019, September 1). How Rosa Parks Helped Spark the Montgomery Bus Boycott. ThoughtCo. https://www.thoughtco.com/rosa-parks-refuses-moving-bus-seat-1779337

Salehin, S. (n.d.). Black Excellence Book Review: "I Know Why The Caged Bird Sings." Uwo.ca. https://uwo.ca/se/thrive/blog/2022/book_review_and_analysis_on_i_know_why_the_caged_bird_sing.html

Sanders, C. R. (2020, February 25). Perspective | Katherine Johnson Should Also Be Remembered for Desegregating Higher Education. Washington Post. https://www.washingtonpost.com/outlook/2020/02/25/katherine-johnson-should-also-be-remembered-desegregating-higher-education/

Scott, M. (2019, April 24). Duke Ellington's Melodies Carried His Message Of Social Justice - UMBC: University Of Maryland, Baltimore County. UMBC. https://umbc.edu/stories/duke-ellingtons-message-of-social-justice/

Silverman, E. (2023, August 28). The 2023 March on Washington is Saturday. Here's what to know. Washington Post. https://www.washingtonpost.com/dc-md-va/2023/08/24/march-on-washington-2023-60th-anniversary-speakers-rally/

Slotnik, D. E. (2019, December 11). Overlooked No More: Bessie Coleman, Pioneering African-American Aviatrix. The New York Times. https://www.nytimes.com/2019/12/11/obituaries/bessie-coleman-overlooked.html

South African History Online. (2013). The Natives Land Act of 1913. Sahistory.org.za. https://www.sahistory.org.za/article/natives-land-act-1913

South African History Online. (2018, July 25). Nelson Rolihlahla Mandela. South African History Online. https://www.sahistory.org.za/people/nelson-rolihlahla-mandela

SparkNotes: I Know Why the Caged Bird Sings: Plot Overview. (2019). Sparknotes.com. https://www.sparknotes.com/lit/cagedbird/summary/

Spring, Dr. K. A. (2017). Biography: Maya Angelou. National Women's History Museum. https://www.womenshistory.org/education-resources/biographies/maya-angelou

ST. FLEUR, N. (2024, January 28). Bessie Coleman. National Geographic Kids. https://kids.nationalgeographic.com/history/article/bessie-coleman

Staff, F. (2021, January 12). Martin Luther King's Civil Disobedience Legacy. FindLaw. https://www.findlaw.com/legalblogs/law-and-life/martin-luther-kings-civil-disobedience-legacy/

Stanford University. (2023). Montgomery Bus Boycott | The Martin Luther King, Jr. Research and Education Institute. Kinginstitute.stanford.edu. https://kinginstitute.stanford.edu/montgomery-bus-boycott

Stauss, J. (2020, February 27). Katherine Johnson: Pioneering NASA mathematician. Space.com. https://www.space.com/katherine-johnson.html

Sympathy Introduction | Shmoop. (n.d.). Www.shmoop.com. https://www.shmoop.com/study-guides/sympathy/

Sympathy. (1899). Poetry Foundation. https://www.poetryfoundation.org/poems/46459/sympathy-56d22658afbc0

Teachout, T. (1996, September 1). (Over)praising Duke Ellington. Commentary Magazine. https://www.commentary.org/articles/terry-teachout/overpraising-duke-ellington/

The 25 Best I Know Why The Caged Bird Sings Quotes. (n.d.). Bookroo.com. https://bookroo.com/quotes/i-know-why-the-caged-bird-sings

The Legacy of Dr. George Washington Carver. (2024, February 20). National Centers for Environmental Information (NCEI). https://www.ncei.noaa.gov/news/legacy-dr-george-washington-carver

The Nobel Peace Prize 1984. (2019). NobelPrize.org. https://www.nobelprize.org/prizes/peace/1984/tutu/biographical/

The Remarkable Life Story of NASA Mathematician Katherine Johnson. (n.d.). Katherine Johnson. https://www.katherinejohnsonfoundation.org/biography/

TOP 25 QUOTES BY HARRIET TUBMAN | A-Z Quotes. (2016). A-Z Quotes. https://www.azquotes.com/author/14834-Harriet_Tubman

Tuskegee University. (2020). George Washington Carver | Tuskegee University. Tuskegee.edu. https://www.tuskegee.edu/support-tu/george-washington-carver

Veliz, L. (2022, April 28). How Did Maya Angelou Get Her Name? Grunge. https://www.grunge.com/846980/how-did-maya-angelou-get-her-name/

Wax, E. (2011, August 23). Martin Luther King's Nonviolent Civil Rights Efforts Still Inspire Across Globe. Washington Post. https://www.washingtonpost.com/lifestyle/style/martin-luther-kings-nonviolent-civil-rights-efforts-still-inspire-across-globe/2011/07/27/gIQA3Nj9YJ_story.html

Who is Rosa Parks? A Glimpse at the Journey of American Activist - ENGLISH TALENT. (2023, September 25). Englishtalent.edu.vn. https://englishtalent.edu.vn/en/who-is-rosa-parks-a-glimpse-at-the-journey-of-american-activist

Winnie Madikizela-Mandela (26 September 1936 – 2 April 2018) – Nelson Mandela Foundation. (2018, April 3). Www.nelsonmandela.org. https://www.nelsonmandela.org/news/entry/winnie-madikizela-mandela-26-september-1936-2-april-2018

www.ingramcontent.com/pod-product-compliance
Lightning Source LLC
Chambersburg PA
CBHW071520120626
46550CB00006B/2288